ALL IS GRIST

ALL IS GRIST

A Book of Essays

BY

G. K. CHESTERTON

Essay Index Reprint Series

BOOKS FOR LIBRARIES PRESS, INC.

FREEPORT, NEW YORK

First published 1932
Reprinted 1967

CONTENTS

ALL IS GRIST

I. ON THE PRUDERY OF SLANG

WHAT puzzles me is that so many things which boast of being wild and free, which are even abused for being wild and free, are in reality rather snobbish, not to say slavish. All that sort of unconventionality seems to me a great deal too conventional. The most obvious and everyday example is the fuss about divorce; which is unfortunately a very everyday example. But the point of divorce is not that people are professing to be reckless, but that people are pretending to be respectable. The point of it is not in the parting of wives and husbands, which has unfortunately happened in various forms in nearly all the various lands and ages. The point of it is the covering of the disunion by the use of the old label of union. Many satirists in many periods have had occasion to note the domestic dissolution that seemed to threaten a social dissolution. Many have had occasion to strike the lyre and lament in the mournful language of Mr. Bentley's Ballade:

> Rupert has bolted with the children's nurse,
> Claude has declared himself an Infidel.

The peculiarity of the recent social tendency is that a visiting-card inscribed "Mr. and Mrs. Rupert" is carefully engraved to cover the fact that the children's nurse is no longer looking after the children. The peculiarity of the position is not that Claude has proclaimed himself an Infidel; but, that Claude has proclaimed himself a Christian with a higher and more purely spiritual religion, which is too exalted to believe in any creeds or sacraments, but which does permit him to remain an ordinary respectable Anglican parson—or possibly even an Anglican bishop.

In all these compromises, it seems to me that the chief feature is the saving of the ordinary social position of the persons involved. And to think first about such social position is not the act of a sceptic but simply of a snob. What matters to a man with a free intelligence is what the man and woman are actually doing, or what the parson or bishop is actually teaching. Whether in the one case somebody gets a new wedding-ring, or in the other case retains an old dog-collar, is surely a matter comparatively conventional. Yet it is at the back of nearly all the pleas for freedom, which profess to be pleas for unconventionality. But there are a great many other examples of this curious contradiction with relation to convention. It appears not only in the manners, but in the language, and especially the slang, of society. There is a queer sort of prudery about slang, and modernity shows it most in what is calls "facing the facts of nature."

For instance, there was a time when it was customary to call a father a father; which seems to me a very normal example of calling a spade a spade. There were, of course, many variations, both formal and familiar, in different times and communities. But most men have used a language as ancient and traditional as that of Esau when he cried aloud, "Hast thou not a blessing for me, O my father?" Now as far as I can discover from the social authorities who tell us all about the Rising Generation and the Bright Young Things, it appears to be considered a mark of advanced intelligence to call your father a bean or a scream, or possibly Tom, Dick, and Harry, in reference (or without reference) to his Christian name. Broadly speaking, the parent of the progressive age appears to answer to "Hi!" or to any loud cry; and it seems to be considered in itself a proof of progress that the cries are very loud indeed. But loud cries do not make any difference to logic; and in this case the logic is all the other way. It is obvious to me that calling the old gentleman "father" is facing the facts of nature. It is also obvious that calling him "bean" is not facing the facts of nature. It is, so far as that example is concerned, perhaps, merely weaving a graceful fairy-tale to cover the facts of nature. It is prettily pretending for a moment that the Heavy Father is an elf of the dimensions of Moth and Mustard-Seed, capable of concealing himself in the green hood of the bean. But that is a digression without being in any way an exception. The general truth obviously is that all these phrases that evade the family relation do therefore evade the facts of life. You may call your father Tom as if he were a total stranger from Australia, whom you had come rather to like at the Empire Club. But in that case it is you who are indulging in a fiction, and ultimately in a convention. The real facts of your relation are rather more remarkable; and to ignore them is to ignore something at once natural and notable. And it is to ignore it in favour of things much more superficial and trivial; the mere society slang or fashion of the passing moment. It is, in fact, to think the rules of the Empire Club more important than the laws of nature. That does not strike me as being natural; to say nothing of being naked. That does not impress me as being realistic, but as being ready to go through any sort of antics rather than face a reality.

There are, indeed, human and historic aspects of this problem, which would in any case be rather too real for our realists to understand. The truth is that traditional humanity has always felt these natural facts to be so real that they were best expressed in some sort of ritual. Talking about them in detail did (and does) very little good; but recognizing them in conduct and courtesy and the very carriage of the body made all men feel sane and near to nature. Men were ceremonial towards their fathers and mothers, just as they were ceremonial about the harvest or the ploughing of the ground or the scattering of the seed. They were ceremonial about these things because these things were so very real; because they are the most real of all realities. They are the things by which we live and without which we die. In the same way, their gleams of simple intelligence enabled them to perceive that their parents were things without which they would never have been alive. The recognition of that fact is entirely realistic, not to say scientific; but the best recognition of it has always been in gesture and artistic form. It has been what I, for one, should unhesitatingly describe as good form.

There are some of the innovators whom I should not expect to understand what is meant by good form. They are far too much tied to convention to understand ritual. They cannot even understand courtesy, so long as the convention of the moment is a convention of discourtesy. But these deplorable people are very rare in any generation; and the majority of the young are doubtless what they always were; and no more than normally disposed to desert normality for the sake of novelty. The trouble is that very few people encourage them really to think about these things, or thrash them out in any intelligent fashion. They are sometimes blamed for not following the conventions of the last generation; to which the obvious answer is that they are following the conventions of this generation. The real trouble is that they are following the conventions far too much. As they have no defence against their fathers except a new fashion, so they will have no defence against their sons except an old fashion. The habit of uttering loud cries (of which I am a warm and enthusiastic supporter) can seldom be carried on absolutely continuously to the age of sixty, without any pause for rest or refreshment. And what is wanted here is not only a pause for refreshment but for reflection. There is a great deal to be said for rapidity; but it is not especially a good way of grasping reality. People merely going the pace, in any age, have generally missed everything except the most artificial and external costume and custom of that age. Men need to walk a little slower to look at the earth and to face the facts of nature.

II. ON LIBERTIES AND LOTTERIES

ALMOST alone among my contemporaries I have not been a sceptic about liberty; but I recognize the materials for scepticism in the discussion about liberties. The difference between the liberties valued by one community and those valued by another is doubtless very great. The vulgar modern argument used against religion, and lately against common decency, would be absolutely fatal to any idea of liberty. It is perpetually said that because there are a hundred religions claiming to be true, it is therefore impossible that one of them should really be true. The argument would appear on the face of it to be illogical, if any one nowadays troubled about logic. It would be as reasonable to say that because some people thought the earth was flat, and others (rather less incorrectly) imagined it was round, and because anybody is free to say that it is triangular or hexagonal, or a rhomboid, therefore it has no shape at all; or its shape can never be discovered; and, anyhow, modern science must be wrong in saying it is an oblate spheroid. The world must be some shape, and it must be that shape and no other; and it is not self-evident that nobody can possibly hit on the right one. What so obviously applies to the material shape of the world equally applies to the moral shape of the universe. The man who describes it may not be right; but it is no argument against his rightness that a number of other people must be wrong.

As I say, the same childish argument is now extended to ordinary morality or decency. It is insisted that, because the decorum of a Roman matron is not exactly the same as that of a Sandwich Islander, therefore there can be no superiority in the one over the other; no possible way of deciding which is the better of the two; and, ultimately, no meaning or value in dignity or propriety at all. The conclusion is so unnatural that, even if the argument were apparently logical, we might be excused for suspecting it of being sophistical. But, as a matter of fact, the argument is not logical enough to be called a sophistry. It is simply transparently untenable; for it rests on the same fallacy: that one man cannot be right because a number of other men are wrong. In this case, of course, it is true that the question is conditioned by different circumstances and that the principle must be applied in different ways. In this case it is true that we cannot say that the whole world is alike, in the sense that we can say that the whole world is round. It is true, but this fashionable argument does not prove it to be true. So far as that argument goes, there might be one costume suitable to all mankind, as there is one custom of washing suitable to all mankind, though some men neglect it and are dirty. All we complain of, in that aspect, is that the sceptic always refuses to be a rationalist.

But the point here is that, if this argument is fatal to faith or modesty, it is a thousand times fatal to liberty. If we simply say that this or that practice is tolerated in this or that place, if we refuse to look for any moral or metaphysical principle by which the differences can be tested, we shall find the definition of liberty dissolving into a dust of differentiations and exceptions. And I very much fear that this is exactly what the definition of liberty will really do. I am very much afraid, as things are going at present, that the next generation will have quite as little idea of what their fathers meant by dying for liberty, as the last generation had of what their fathers meant by dying for religion or sound theology or the true faith. There is already a large number of modern writers who talk as if the old notion of independence, national or personal, were something simply inconceivable as well as impossible; exactly as the champions of liberty, a hundred years ago, spoke of the mysterious dogmas of the Church. Indeed, it is quite as easy, by the methods of the rationalistic heckler, to suggest that freedom is nonsense as that faith is nonsense. It is a great deal too easy. That is what made me suspect it from the first in both cases. But, anyhow, it is perfectly true that variation gives the sceptic an opportunity in both cases. It is easy to show that liberties are local; it is much less easy to prove that liberty is universal.

For instance, I am writing these words in a country which many of my countrymen regard as utterly crushed by a system destructive of every liberty. There is no doubt that Italy has restrained the liberty of the Press; it can easily be argued that it has restrained the liberty of the people. But it is quite certain that the people enjoy, and take for granted, quite definite forms of liberty that do not exist in England at all. The Italians would think Mussolini was mad if he forbade lotteries, as the English law forbids lotteries. It would seem to them very much what forbidding lawn tennis would seem to us. The whole Latin world regards the notion of not being allowed to drink beer between three and six very much as we should regard the idea of not being allowed to eat buns on Tuesdays and Thursdays. It is quite inadequate to call it tyranny: because they would call it lunacy. Now I have argued often enough upon these points elsewhere, and I am not going to dwell on these particular points now. I am merely using them to point out that, even where we imagine there is a clear-cut issue against liberty, there is a considerable complexity when we come to argue about liberties. If the costume of the Sandwich Islander is an argument against abstract decency, then certainly the liberty of the lottery is an argument against abstract liberty. If the thousand and one religions make a case against religion, then the thousand and one liberties make a case against liberty. And I am very much afraid that, in the present mood of mankind, that case may carry weight. It will be very useful to the monopolist, or modern tyrant, who carries most weight in the modern world; and when he has taken away all English freedom from the Englishman and all Italian freedom from the Italian, he will smile broadly and say that, after all, men have never agreed about the definition of being free.

I am so paradoxical as to think that there is a real theory of freedom. Perhaps I may have a shot at expounding it in another essay. But the theory is bound to be rather theoretical; and the modern world, having tried in vain to be thoughtful, has fallen back on the abject alternative of being practical. And it looks to me as if liberty would suffer in that practical age much more than religion suffered in the age of the French Revolution. It can easily be derided, quite as successfully as Victorian decorum or the legend of Mrs. Grundy. But just as there are other kinds of decorum besides Victorian decorum, and yet a sense of dignity and decency behind them all, so there can be other kinds of freedom besides that of the free-born Englishman, and yet leave an ultimate significance in the ideal of being free. Broadly, I should say that the commonwealth is healthy in which all things are *not* common, but some things, in the exact sense of the phrase, "distinguished." Many who talk about distinction mean only aristocratic distinction; and by that mean only fashion. But fashion is almost the opposite of distinction. A democracy can be distinguished, if its citizens are distinguishable; if each has an area of choice in which he really chooses. To keep that area of choice as large as possible is the real function of freedom. But, as there is no space here for me to develop my eleutheromaniac dogma on this page, I feel inclined to ask my readers to do it for me; or at least to think it out for themselves. I dare not offer a prize; I understand it is now likely to be classed with a lottery. And it would be dreadful if free-born Englishmen were allowed to do what is permitted to Italian slaves. But if any one thinks he has a definition that will save liberty, I should be interested . . . and, I will add, surprised.

III. ON THE NUDISTS

In a great many illustrated papers there is a continuous and by this time rather monotonous stream of articles and illustrations advertising the new Gymnosophists of Germany. I mean the cult of cranks who insist in a crazy degree on certain notions connected with sun-cures; to me, more suggestive of sunstroke. An occasional article about them might be normal enough in any magazine, as being in the nature of a news-item. But the concentrated attempt to boom this barbaric sophistry is not a good sign of the turn of public opinion, and seems connected with that particular sort of glorification of the body which generally goes with a certain weakness in the head. There is, indeed, something singularly weak-minded about the sort of respect—we might almost say reverence—with which experiments of this sort are often described in our journalism. It seems quite sufficient to insist upon the seriousness of any persons engaged in such experiments, a seriousness which invariably marks faddists and fanatics and small provincial sects of every kind. Thus the admiring advertiser explains how very solemnly the German professor plays the goat, though not quite so seriously as a real goat. For goats do not laugh at anything, least of all at themselves, and in this the nature-worshippers in question are undoubtedly, as they would say, at one with nature. Nature is inferior to man in many things, but most of all in respect of the human specialty of humour. For the rest, goatishness has often been made a sort of symbol of paganism; but even among the pagans it was not regarded as the highest form of paganism. "Half a beast is the great god Pan," as the poet very truly observed; and the satyr and the faun were conceived as being half-human and half-goatish, presumably on the principle that half a goat is better than no beastliness. To a serene and philosophical judgment, it will not appear altogether inappropriate that, in the division of mankind, the goats were on the wrong side of the judgment seat.

But the fallacy in such a fashion is concerned with a certain ultimate common sense about mankind. The cult of nakedness, which used to be called the Adamite Heresy, does, in fact, reveal its falsity at the beginning, even in the merely material aspect. Man is not independent of artificial things, even in the most natural sense. Nakedness is not even practical, except on selected occasions that are entirely artificial. Even the physical conditions of the world bear witness to something in man that is strictly to be called metaphysical, that is unique and detached and raised above the obvious physical order. It is not native to man to go without clothes, unless it is native to man to die of double pneumonia in about a month. He cannot do it at all through the greater part of the year, or over the greater part of the globe. And the very fact that he has been left, as it were, without any aids to survival except what we call artificial aids, is a proof that in his case they can hardly even be called artificial. It is not a question so much of artificiality which departs from nature, but rather of art, which is the essence of human nature; art, which is almost the nature of man.

For instance, man could not exist at all, in the ordinary sense, if he had not discovered the dreadful and astonishing thing that is called fire. It would be just as easy to elaborate a philosophy against fire as a philosophy against clothes. In fact, the two things often serve the same purpose, but fire is by far the more questionable and dangerous of the two. It is not very often that a man is actually killed by a hat or tortured by a pair of trousers. There was, indeed, an instrument of torture called the Boot; it was used in seventeenth-century Scotland, and we hear a great deal about it when it was used by Royalists upon Whigs, and very little about it when it was afterwards used by Whigs upon Royalists. But even those who complain most of what Mr. H. G. Wells called the Misery of Boots would hardly compare it to being sentenced to the Boot, and certainly not to being sentenced to the fire. Yet it would be easy enough, in the accepted style of rhetoric about these things, to represent every advocate of ordinary warmth as invoking some such unnatural peril. All fuel would, in the medieval phrase, smell of the faggot. To defend the stove would be to defend the stake; and any housewife lighting a fire would be re-lighting the fires of Smithfield. Such talk would be no more ridiculous than many of the ravings of the reformers, who cry out that they are being persecuted as by the Spanish Inquisition when they are required to wear common human clothes. There would be any number of other ways of giving the familiar element a permanent flavour of arson. Where, is it alleged, is Woman most oppressed and tormented; where is she enslaved and threatened with every type of tribal and ancestral brutality? Where but at the fireside? A little confused oratory and imagery, applied to that notion, would be quite enough to suggest a general idea that the woman was to be roasted like a leg of mutton. Indeed, the whole business of cookery would afford a most convenient and fitting parallel. Cooking is artificial, exactly as clothes are artificial. Some people do largely dispense with cookery, as some people do frequently dispense with clothes. There are prigs who live on nuts, as there are prigs who live in nakedness. But there are a good many other human beings as well, and most of them are of opinion that cookery is a part of something which we call culture. And, while we may argue for ever about whether it is natural, most of us know that it is normal.

The whole conception of culture is bound up with that first fact about man; that he is not himself, until he has added to himself certain things which are, in a sense, outside himself. As he is more powerful than any other creature with those things, so he is more helpless than any other creature without those things. It would be easy for the wild philosopher to argue that the very existence of fire is an insult to sunlight. It would be easy for him to denounce Prometheus as the rival of Apollo. I can imagine him elaborately explaining, in an endless series of lectures, that we ought not to need any such indirection or deflection of the rays of the sun; that we ought never to have come into a condition in which the sun's rays are not sufficient to us; that it is an insult to the splendid solar unity to tear away flames from it, like rags from a golden garment. It is true that, as a minor matter of fact, the sun's rays are not always there at all. But that is just as much an objection to the attack on clothes as to the attack on cooking. The point is that the whole of this philosophy is wrong at the root; is wrong in its whole conception of the nature and position of man on the earth; is wrong even in its relation to matter; and is wrong long before we come to the higher question of morals.

But when we do come to it, we shall not be surprised to find that the theory is as false in moral fact as it is in material fact. A human being is not even completely human without clothes, because they have become a part of him as the symbol of purely human things; of dignity, of modesty, of self-ownership, of property, and privacy and honour. Even in the purely artistic sense humanity would never have become human without them, because the range of self-expression and symbolic decoration would have been hopelessly limited, and there would have been no outlet even for the most primary instincts about colour and form. The Adamite heresy begins in madness, but it ends only in monotony. Some actually praise it because they think it would dull and blunt all sorts of human feelings, fancies, and shades of sentiment; and they are the sort of madmen who would actually boast of monotony. But the central civilization of mankind is not very likely to be deeply disturbed, in its immemorial intellectual instincts, by these crudities on the borderland. It takes a long time to explain such simple things; but, when a man disregards them, it is a shorter way to laugh at him and lock him up.

IV. ON BUSINESS EDUCATION

A LONG time ago I pointed out the fallacy of crying out for a practical man. I noted, what should be obvious enough, that when a problem is really bad and basic, we should rather wail and pray and cry aloud for an unpractical man. The practical man only knows the machine in practice; just as many a man can drive a motor-car who could not mend it, still less design it. The more serious is the trouble, the more probable it is that some knowledge of scientific theory will be required; and though the theorist will be called unpractical, he will probably be also indispensable. What is generally meant by a business man is a man who knows the way in which our particular sort of modern business does generally work. It does not follow that he is imaginative enough to suggest something else, when it obviously does not work. And (unless I very much misread the signs of the modern transition) we are soon coming to a time when everybody will be looking for somebody who can suggest something else.

I am glad to see that what I applied to the unpractical reformer has been applied, by an unimpeachably practical man, to the unpractical instructor. Mr.

John C. Parker, a hundred-per-cent American, a highly successful engineer, the vigorous agent of a company named after Edison—in short, a man with all the unquestioned stigmata of a Regular Guy, rigorous and energetic in the application of science to business, has recently astonished his friends by delivering an address with the truly admirable title, "Wanted—An Unpractical Education." I have only read his remarks in an indirect form, but they seem to me quite excellent remarks. "My complaint would be rather that training youth to earn a living is not education at all; second, that a specific training may keep the youngster from earning the best kind of living; and third, that it can't be done in school anyhow." Or, again, "I would infinitely prefer that education fit him for happiness and decency in poverty, than for wealth acquired through the sacrifice of himself and his character." These are almost startlingly sensible counsels; though what they would look like side by side with those shiny and strenuous advertisements inscribed "You Can Add Ten Thousand Dollars to Your Salary," or "This Man Trebled His Turnover in Two Weeks," it is not my province to conjecture.

But this extraordinary affair called Business Education, which has begun to be supported in England after having long subsisted in America, has another aspect perhaps not so easy to explain. When I say that we want to train the citizen and not the city man, or the equivocal "something in the city," I mean even more than Mr. Parker's just and rational ideal of "the fitting of students to live richly and fully and contribute most broadly to the welfare of the social group who have paid for their education." Being myself a senile survival of the old republican idealism (I use the adjective to express the American political principle, not the American political party) I mean something else, as well as the mere social enjoyment of culture. I mean that to train a citizen is to train a critic. The whole point of education is that it should give a man abstract and eternal standards, by which he can judge material and fugitive conditions. If the citizen is to be a reformer, he must start with some ideal which he does not obtain merely by gazing reverently at the unreformed institutions. And if any one asks, as so many are asking: "What is the use of my son learning all about ancient Athens and remote China and medieval guilds and monasteries, and all sorts of dead or distant things, when he is going to be a superior scientific plumber in Pimlico?" the answer is obvious enough. "The use of it is that he may have some power of comparison, which will not only prevent him from supposing that Pimlico covers the whole planet, but also enable him, while doing full credit to the beauties and virtues of Pimlico, to point out that, here and there, as revealed by alternative experiments, even Pimlico may conceal somewhere a defect."

Now, the nuisance of all this notion of Business Education, of a training for certain trades, whether of plumber or plutocrat, is that they will *prevent* the intelligence being sufficiently active to criticize trade and business properly. They begin by stuffing the child, not with the sense of justice by which he can judge the world, but with the sense of inevitable doom or dedication by which he must accept that particular very worldly aspect of the world. Even while he is a baby he is a bank-clerk, and accepts the principles of banking which Mr. Joseph Finsbury so kindly explained to the banker. Even in the nursery he is an actuary or an accountant; he lisps in numbers and the numbers come. But he cannot *criticize* the principles of banking, or entertain the intellectual fancy that the modern world is made to turn too much on a Pythagorean worship of Numbers. But that is because he has never heard of the Pythagorean philosophy; or, indeed, of any other philosophy. He has never been taught to think, but only to count. He lives in a cold temple of abstract calculation, of which the pillars are columns of figures. But he has no basic sense of Comparative

Religion (in the true sense of that tiresome phrase), by which he may discover whether he is in the right temple, or distinguish one temple from another. This is bad enough when we are dealing with the normal sense of number and quantity, the eternal foundations of rational and permanent commerce; which are in themselves as pure and abstract as Pythagoras. It becomes both preposterous and perilous when we are dealing with the mere scramble of speculation and economic illusion which is called business in America and elsewhere; with all its degrading publicity, with all its more dangerous secrecy. To begin a boy's training by teaching him to admire these things, and then call it Business Education, is exactly like teaching him to worship Baal and Baphomet, and then calling it Religious Education. And much of what is called commercial training is really of this character. Stevenson, with the assistance of Lloyd Osbourne (himself an American), gives a very vivid and amusing sketch of it in *The Wrecker*. His American hero very justly resents being laughed at merely because he leaves the *u* out of "colour"; but adds that his critics might have had a better case had they known that his father "had paid large sums to have him brought up in a gambling-hell."

Anyhow, that is what is the matter with Business Education; that it narrows the mind; whereas the whole object of education is to broaden the mind; and especially to broaden it so as to enable it to criticize and condemn such narrowness. Everybody ought to learn first a general view of the history of man, of the nature of man, and (as I, for one, should add) of the nature of God. This may enable him to consider the rights and wrongs of slavery in a slave community, of cannibalism in a cannibal community, or of commerce in a commercial community. If he is immediately initiated into the mysteries of these institutions themselves, if he is sworn in infancy to take them as seriously as they take themselves, if he becomes a trader not only before he becomes a traveller, but even before he becomes a true citizen of his own town, he will never be able to denounce those institutions—or even to improve them. Such a state will never have the ideas or imagination to reform itself; and hustle and bustle and business activity will have resulted in the dead fixity of a fossil.

V. ON THE INTELLECT OF YESTERDAY

Is the present generation better educated than the last generation? Is it more intelligent than any one of any number of past generations? Most of those writing on the subject say "Yes." Most of them, by a curious coincidence, belong to the present generation, or some very recent generation. I have no axe to grind in the matter; neither the ancestral axe of Brutus, red with the blood of his sons, nor the latest pattern of guillotine on which a revolutionary son can enthusiastically execute his father. There are some matters in which the world has lately veered towards my own opinions; some matters in which it has turned away from them. But I have enough intellectual curiosity to have doubts, and certainly enough to make distinctions.

I think there would be a case for maintaining this: that the world has improved in everything *except* intellect. In artistic sensibilities, and even in social sympathies (at least, of a certain kind), I think there has been a quickening and a response. I think it probable that the number of people who can rapidly get used to a foreign fashion or style of ornament, who can guess what an eccentric artist is driving at, who can feel the emotions evoked by unusual music, is larger than it was in mid-Victorian times. But these things do not appeal to the intellect. And I think they appeal to the modern mood because they do not appeal to the intellect. They make signals to the sentimental part of human nature, and the code of those signals is learned more quickly than it would once have been. But when it comes to anything like a strain on the intellect as such, I think that most modern people are much stupider than those in the age of my father, and probably very much stupider than those in the age of my grandfather. I have reasons for my belief, but it illustrates my point that the modern reader would hardly listen to a long process of reasoning. I believe I could even prove it, if people now were patient enough to listen to proof.

First, it must be realized that liveliness in the preacher does not mean liveliness in the congregation. On the contrary, the extreme liveliness in the preacher is produced by dullness in the congregation. I am ready to believe, for instance, that Mr. Lloyd George is a more purely entertaining speaker than Cobden. But that is because Mr. Lloyd George speaks to men who want to be entertained. Cobden spoke to men who wanted to be convinced. The listeners provided something of the liveliness needed to carry them through a purely logical process. When there was a congregation of logicians, as there was in some of the old Scottish Calvinist kirks, the preacher could reckon on being followed when his discourse was a pure demonstration in logic. It is when the congregation is dull that it wants to be amused. Cobden stood for various views which I do not myself find convincing; but his audience was convinced, it was not merely amused. Now, a man cannot be convinced by an argument without following the argument. He can be amused, even if he goes to sleep in the middle of the argument and wakes up just in time to hear a joke about Tories drinking beer or Bolshevists sharing boots. I believe there is infinitely less of this intellectual *attention* to an argument than there used to be.

It is illustrated, for instance, in the great modern change in the Press. I am not now arguing about whether Lord Northcliffe's revolution in journalistic methods was morally or socially good. I only say it may well stand for something which is intellectually very much to the bad. When I was a boy, the papers printed long and detailed reports of speeches by Gladstone or Goschen or Asquith, on complex controversies of economics and finance. Perhaps they were not worth printing; perhaps they were not worth reading; but they were read. Now, it may be very bright and pleasant to have all Gladstone's subtle and searching logical distinctions swept away in favour of the fixed and unfailing headline of "What Did Mr. Gladstone Say in 1885?' It may be very comfortable to forget all the luminous legal distinctions of Asquith, and agree that that statesman never said anything in his life except "Wait and See." But it is not a proof of increased intellectual activity that we are satisfied with the simple and soothing quotations. The minds of our fathers may have been occupied in futile and pedantic hair-splitting, but their minds were really capable of splitting a hair. It may be more cosy to be stunned with a blow on the head by a club than to have one of your hairs split by a needle, but it is not any better tribute to the quality of your head, or of anybody else's.

Or take another test from another type of inquiry. When all the drawing-rooms began to buzz suddenly with the name of Einstein, some of us were enabled to guess that they must once have buzzed quite as abruptly with the name of Darwin. Some of us are inclined to guess that Darwinism became a fashion long before anybody really thought it was a fact. Doubtless any number of society ladies went about saying that Professor Darwin was really too wonderful, just as they afterwards went about saying that Professor Einstein was really too wonderful. But, when all is said, there is no comparison between the two cases. Any number of people did really attack the study of biology, in order to agree or disagree with Darwin. Hardly one person in a thousand thought of attacking the higher mathematics in order to agree with Einstein. People did talk about Darwinism as well as about Darwin. Most of those who talk about Einstein talk about Einstein. They know nothing but the name and the notion that something very important has happened in connexion with the name. The talk about Darwin may have been popular science, but it was science, and it was popular. The talk about Einstein may rather be called popular nescience. He has not made astronomy really popular, as the other made biology really popular. And I believe that the reason is a certain increased laziness of the intellect; that fewer people are ready for a long, sustained logical demonstration, quite apart from whether we think that the demonstration really demonstrates. In my boyhood there were any number of funny little atheists running about ready and eager to *prove* what they had learned from the work of Darwin. So there were any number of fanatical little Free-Traders eager to *prove* what they had learned from the speeches of Cobden. I do not find men now so eager to prove things; but, at the most, to assure me that they have been proved.

One way of putting it is that this is a psychological age, which is the opposite of an intellectual age. It is not a question of persuading men, but of suggesting how they are persuaded. It is an age of Suggestion; that is, of appeal to the irrational part of man. Men discussed whether Free Trade was false or true; they do not so much discuss whether Empire Free Trade is false or true, as whether it is booming or slumping; whether it is based on an understanding of Mass Psychology, or whether its opponents or supporters have what Americans call Personality. It is all great fun, and there is doubtless a truth in it, as in other things. But, whatever else it is, it is not a mark of stronger mentality, and any old Scotch Calvinist farmer, who could follow his minister's desolate and appalling sermon to Seventeenthly and Lastly, had an immeasurably better brain.

VI. ON TRAVEL'S SURPRISES

TRAVELLERS' tales are supposed to be tall tales; but I have always found them fall short. I have nearly always felt that the real monument or landscape, when I saw it for myself, was something stranger and more striking than the indirect impression of reading. The old tale against travellers' tales was that they magnified everything; that every lizard became a dragon and every savage tribe a race of giants. But my experience is that travellers in a strange land, especially if they have travelled in it long, tend too much to forget its strangeness. They become concerned with a dust of details, and tend to take the green lizards as casually as the green leaves. The danger is rather, I think, that a man can live in a tribe of gigantic savages, and grow to remark and record all sorts of details about their tribal taxes or their coinage of tusks or hides, and, at the end of his detailed narrative, forget even to mention that they were giants. For as there are things too big and obvious to be noticed, so especially there are things too big and obvious to be remembered.

There have, indeed, been many cases in which

travellers have been accused of telling lies, which have often afterwards turned out to be truths. Modern research, which has justified so many medieval reputations, has made some reparation even to medieval travellers. It was Marco Polo, I think, who reported that he had met in Africa men who had the heads of dogs. And most modern critics treated it as a manifest fairy-tale, as if he claimed to have seen birds with the heads of elephants. But it is very likely indeed that the traveller saw baboons, or some of the larger apes; and his description is really more scientific and exact than the common popular impression about men and monkeys. For the higher apes have not that sort of hollow, half-human visage which we see in the little monkeys; they often have an aggressive and solid projection of nose and jaw, like the nozzle or muzzle of a dog. But even here the principle of comparison is true. It is one thing to read in a book about dog-headed men and believe it or not as we choose; it must have been quite another to see the first of the huge hairy anthropoids—monstrous, mysterious, erect; a premature provocation to the myth of the Missing Link. And I repeat that foreign sights have mostly affected me as the first ape must have affected the first explorer; not necessarily as something beautiful or charming, but certainly as something very surprising and entirely unexpected.

When I first saw St. Mark's, Venice, I am by no means sure that I liked it; but I am quite sure that I was surprised by it; that it was not only quite different from anything I had ever seen, but quite different from anything I had ever expected. I thought it looked like Aladdin's Palace in a pantomime. And the impression was not altogether false; for a man standing in that great merchant city of the Western Mediterranean is, by a paradox, standing deep in the golden gate of the East. There was always something a little too Oriental about the Venetian republic; and this, it has been suggested, was why it did, in a sense, fall like Carthage rather than survive like Rome. But, however that may be, the Christian who first looks at the Christian Church of St. Mark's is as startled as if it were a Chinese pagoda. Yet I had often seen pictures of it; photographs, and even coloured photographs; but these never conveyed how extraordinary the thing really is. For the extraordinary thing is that anything so fantastic should be solid.

The queer thing is that what one would expect to be the first thing mentioned is generally the last thing mentioned. I had heard a thousand things about Jerusalem ever since my babyhood, and seen views of it, and plans of it, and read controversies about it. But, somehow or other, I had never got hold of the first fact that it is a mountain city. A city that is set upon a hill cannot be hid; but somehow it seems as if the hill could be hid. All the photographs and descriptions I had seen were like glimpses of an Eastern bazaar; and suggested all the accompaniments of heat and stagnation and flat desert sands. Whereas the real city, relatively speaking, is much more like a castle on the crags of the Rhine, or set high among the rocks of Spain. From Spain itself it would be easy to take similar examples. I knew that the Escorial was a palace; I did not know that it looks much more like a prison; but especially I did not know the strange journey into the mountains by which it is reached, with the consequent sense of separation and unearthly loneliness in that huge habitation of a moody King. In short, I have sometimes positively disliked the famous spectacles of travel. But the thing I disliked was always utterly different from the thing that I was expected to like; so utterly different that I generally came at last to like it.

I had another experience of the same sort recently; I suddenly saw Canada. I had visited it before; but I had never seen it before. On the former occasion I crossed the frontier from the United States; and there is nothing particularly interesting about the frontier except the undignified fuss about Prohibition. On the second occasion I went up the St. Lawrence to Montreal. This also was a thing I had heard of often enough; but nothing I had ever heard of gave me any rumour of the reality. As is usual in such cases, the *point* of the experience is almost always missed. The point of the experience is that the traveller is carried far northward, almost as if he were going to the North Pole, or at least to find the North-West Passage. He sees icebergs and the Northern Lights and the whales of the northern waters; a hundred signs recall to him the Arctic adventures of which he read as a boy. Then the ship takes a sharp turn, which seems like one of the sharpest turns in navigation, and enters a new, an enormous, and yet a secret world. He feels, as the first explorers must have felt, that it is really a world set apart; that he had never guessed the earth contained anything so vast yet so concealed. And the impression is now increased when there begin to appear upon the narrowing coasts of that inland sea, villages and the spires of churches that are not altogether like anything he has left behind. It is as if there were another Mediterranean, with another civilization in all its ports and shrines. So a man sails up the great St. Lawrence, wondering more and more, until the broad river seems to split about the great rock of Quebec.

I fancied that there might be here the beginning and the end of a quarrel I remember in my youth. Mr. Rudyard Kipling wrote a poem in praise of Canada, which very much annoyed the Canadians. Many of them stated with great sternness that, if he praised them any more, they would give him a good hard knock. The ground of the offence was that he had referred to the Dominion of Canada as "Our Lady of the Snows." This was held to imply that Canada has no local industry except snowballing; that her principal exports are icebergs; and that the typical Canadian citizen is a sort of furry and inarticulate Eskimo. One Canadian poet haughtily replied that Canada contained glowing maple woods in which England might be lost. One Canadian painter painted an ironical allegory, representing the spirit of the Dominion sitting on a pile of gorgeous fruits and varied products of the sun, and entitled the picture, "Our Lady of the Snows." I am no Imperialist in particular, but the days of my skirmishes with Mr. Kipling about Imperialism are long past, and I am affected by the thought of leaving Mr. Kipling and Canada in an embrace of reconciliation. I would therefore suggest that the impression of Arctic magnificence may be partly due to the fact that, though Canada is not made of snow, in a sense her gates are of ice. And though her woods are really as beautiful as any Canadian painter or poet can depict them, the true traveller really does have an impression of having travelled beyond the North Pole to find them.

VII. ON FLOCKING

THE elusive, enormous, and nameless thing, with which I have so long wrestled, as with a slippery leviathan, in such places as this, suddenly heaved in sight the other day and took on a sort of formless form. I am always getting these brief glimpses of the monster, though they seldom last long enough for me to make head or tail of it. In this case it appeared in a short letter to the *Daily Express,* which ran, word for word, as follows:

"In reply to your article 'What Youth Wants in Church,' I assert that it does not want sadness, ceremony, or humbug. Youth wants to know only about the present and future, not about what happened 2,000 years ago. If the churches forsake these things, young people will flock to them."

The syntax is a little shaky, and the writer does not mean that the young people will flock to the things that happened 2,000 years ago if only the churches will desert them. He does actually mean (what is much more extraordinary) that the young people will flock to the churches merely because the churches have forsaken all the original objects of their existence. Every feature of every church, from a cross on a spire to an old hymn-book left in a pew, refers more or less to certain things that happened about 2,000 years ago. If we do not want to be reminded of those things, the natural inference is that we do not want any of the buildings built to remind us of them. So far from flocking to them, we shall naturally desire to get away from them; or still more to clear them away. But I cannot understand why something which is unpopular because of what it means should become frightfully popular because it no longer means anything. A War Memorial is a memorial of the war, and I can imagine that those who merely hate the memory might merely hate the memorial. But what would be the sense of saying that, if only all the names of the dead were scraped off the War Memorials, huge pilgrimages would be made from all the ends of the earth to visit and venerate the absence of names on a memorial of nothing?

Most of us would not devote our short summer holiday to visiting the ruin of what had once been the record of something that we did not want to think about. Nor would most people, indifferent to the Christian origin of Christian churches, waste their time in churches merely because they had ceased to be Christian. There are plenty of other places in which to spend our holidays, and plenty of other resorts to which young people can flock, without flocking to hollow shrines stripped of all traces of their history or their object. He would be a bold spirit who should hope to lure the duchess back from the Lido, or the typist from the seaside sun-cure, by offering to show them a chapel of no particular date, with no particular design, in which a total stranger had promised not to mention something that happened 2,000 years ago. Somehow I do not think there would be a flock of duchesses, or even typists, at the doors of that weirdly negative edifice. And this marks the first of the fallacies which beset this rather fashionable style of protest or proposal. Even supposing it were true that theology is unpopular, it does not follow that the absence of theology is popular. This need no more be true of the absence of theology than of the absence of conchology or bacteriology, or anything else. I may not want to hear a bore talking about bimetallism, but it does not follow that I want to go for a walking tour with the bore when he promises not to mention bimetallism. I may not wish to listen to the lecture on "Genetics and Genesis" at the Co-educational Congress at Gum Springs, Ill., but neither do I want to go to the Co-educational Congress at Gum Springs, or anywhere else, even if there is to be no lecture on "Genetics and Genesis." And surely those who are so innocently confident of the attraction of merely negative religion might realize that a broad-minded parson can be as much of a bore about nothing as anybody can be about anything.

But there is another, more subtle, more sunken and fundamental queerness about this way of looking at things. As I have said before, it is only occasionally that we get a real glimpse of its strange outline, as we get it for a moment in this letter. The minds of these people work backwards, from effect to cause, and not from cause to effect. The cause of the Church, the cause which produced it, the cause for which it stands, is regarded as something bad, something that ought to be abolished. In that case, one would naturally infer that the Church ought to be abolished. But this type of thinker does not begin with the cause; he begins with the result, and then turns on the cause and rends it, as if the cause were a disfigurement that had been added afterwards to the result. He suggests that the result must destroy its cause, and go off looking for another cause, in the hope of becoming the result of something else. It is as if the Union Jack were wandering about the world trying to mean the dragon standard of the Sacred Emperor of China, or the Blue Peter were bending all its efforts to become a flag of truce with the significance of the White Flag.

One explanation is that such people, who commonly call themselves progressive, are in the most stodgy sense conservative. They cannot bear to alter any concrete fact, but only the idea behind it. They cannot actually abolish the Union Jack or the White Flag, but only all that they stand for. So they see in front of them a solid block of brick called a church. They accept that; they cannot conceive a real revolt against that; they are even ready to throw themselves into all sorts of schemes for making this mere brick building fashionable, so that people shall "flock" to it. It commands their strange loyalty in its own strange way, merely by being there. It is a solid fact; something must be done with it; and therefore something must be done for it. In pure reason, it is about as reasonable as saying that since we have a Post Office we had better turn it into a swimming-bath, or that the successful establishment of a tennis court necessitates our using it as a turnip field. But the practical man does not trouble about pure reason; he can confront, with an unsmiling visage, what is in reality pure unreason. For pure reason involves some degree of imagination, and not only creative but also destructive imagination. The thinker must not only be able to think things, but to unthink them; he must be imaginative enough to unimagine anything.

Now this sort of conservative cannot unthink anything that is perceptible to his senses. He can only unthink the theory on which it depends, because it is only a theory. He cannot unimagine the big brick church in front of him, as it actually bulks in the landscape. He cannot imagine the landscape without the church; he can only imagine the church without the religion, or the religion without the reason. In the world of ideas he can alter anything, however fundamental, as if it were something fanciful. But he cannot be fanciful about a fact like a brick building; that is a solid object, and must be made a solid success. People must be induced to "flock" to it, even if it has to be turned into an aquarium or an aerodrome. In one sense, to do him justice, this melancholy materialist is the most disinterested of men. The mystic is one who will serve something invisible for his own reasons. The materialist is one who will serve anything visible for no reason. But there are a good many of him, and, even if he has not begun to flock very much into the churches of the present and future, he does already flock a good deal in the correspondence columns of the newspapers.

VIII. ON THE BEHAVIOURIST

EVERYBODY knows that a new school of sceptics has recently appeared, especially in America; they call themselves the Behaviourists, and the late Mr. Harvey Wickham called them the Misbehaviourists. So far as I can understand, their philosophy is rooted in a theory of physiology: the theory that thought is originally a sort of movement of the body rather than the brain. "There is nothing in the brain," I think one of them has written, "except a lot of neurons. We do not think with our minds. We think with our muscles." Those of us, that is, who are so old-fashioned as to think at all. For we have all seen vigorous representatives of the rising generation who suppose that everything can be done with the muscles, and whom nobody, not even a psychologist of the far-off nineteenth century, would accuse of merely using their minds. I am not especially concerned with the truth or falsehood of this fancy. While it is flourished, like the majority of such fancies, with a vague defiance directed towards orthodoxy or tradition, it really has no sort of importance for them. It is an excellent example of the rule about nearly all such new notions that are valued as new negations. The new scientific theory never does really deny the old religious theory. What it does do is to deny—or, rather, destroy—the old scientific theory. And it was precisely in the name of that old theory that religion was once to have been destroyed. The heretics never attack orthodoxy; the heretics only avenge orthodoxy on each other.

It does not matter to any Christian whether God has made a man to think with his brains or his big toe. But it did matter very much to the recent type of Materialist that a man could only think with his brains. He was perpetually basing all sorts of destructive arguments on an analysis of what he called the convolutions and the "matter" in the brain. He was as devoted as M. Hercule Poirot to The Little Grey Cells; but, alas! with far less brilliant and entertaining results. All that the Behaviourist does is, in every sense, to dash out the brains of the old Materialist. There is no question of his touching the soul, even the soul of an old Materialist, for that escapes him as completely as it does every other kind of material analysis, including that of the old Materialist himself. What he abolishes is not the soul, but the cells on which his predecessor depended for the denial of the soul. If ever we do really come to talk about a brilliant idea flashing through our biceps, or a curious and original theory creeping up the calf of our leg, it may sound to some a little funny, or even fantastic. It will not make the slightest difference to those who believe that God made an invisible spirit as part of an invisible order. But it *will* make nonsense of pages and pages of recent realistic literature, in which the crumbling grey matter proved that nothing but death awaited even the primary form of mind, or in which the soul was supposed to have been tracked to its lair and killed in a cell under the cavern of the skull. Libraries of nineteenth-century scepticism would become so much lumber; but the mystical passage in St. Paul about the glorified body would not be in the least affected either way. It would be amusing to irreverent persons if men ever began to look for the Differential Calculus in their deltoid muscles or to conceal a joke somewhere near the joint of the elbow. But it would only contradict the man who said that all truths were in the human skull or all jokes a decay of brain-stuff; not the man who says that jokes come from man, or that man and mathematical truths come from God.

Nevertheless, there is another aspect of this fancy, whether or no it is anything more than a fancy, in which it may be used to suggest a rather neglected truth. If we were only allowed to accept scientific suggestions, as jokes, we could sometimes get some serious good out of them. If the young scientist would ever allow us to regard his hypothesis as anything so human as a half-truth, it might sometimes really be worth while to find the other half. If, instead of claiming that everything is covered by his explanation, he confined himself to pleading that there is something in his suggestion, he would look considerably less of a fool when the next man, with the new explanation, comes along in about thirty years. And there is something in the suggestion about mind and muscle, though there may be nothing but nonsense in an attempt to affirm muscle and deny mind. It is true, I think, that among the lesser guides to truth is a certain craving for creative movement: a longing to stretch the limbs, to smite, to scrawl, to make sweeping gestures, to lift up the hands as well as the heart. There is an instinctive movement of the body towards better and nobler things, as in the text that said, "I will lift up mine eyes to the hills," or in that divine command of liberation that took the form of "Stretch forth thine hand." The old ceremonial gestures of the human body are necessary to the health of the human soul: the gesture that pledged the guest in the goblet; that strewed the flowers upon the grave; that drew the sword for the salute or set up the candle before the shrine. In that sense a man actually can think with his muscles; he can pray with his muscles; he can love with his muscles and lament with his muscles. All religion that is without that gesture, all Puritan or purely Intellectualist religion that rages at ritual, is raging at human nature. If an ancient pagan came from the city of Plato and the temple of Pallas, and found himself in a certain type of town of the Middle West, I admit that he would probably prefer to be a Behaviourist rather than a Baptist.

Now, if we take a fine poem of religious invocation, like that which Chaucer called his ABC, which consists of a series of apostrophes to the Virgin, each like the first salute at morning, we shall feel the almost physical presence of this sort of ancient or medieval Behaviourism. The words seem to carry with them a gesture; it is impossible not to feel that the poet is doing something; is bowing to a lady or standing up to salute a sovereign; is lifting an offering up or casting an offering down. Such an opening as "Almighty and all-mercyable Queen" has a breadth about it beyond that of the brain, in the narrow sense, because such invocation is, among other things, one of the most ancient human habits of the body. Of course, that broad and expansive gesture can be found in other poets besides Chaucer, and other schools besides Chaucer's. But it has not expanded with the particular modern type of expansion. Milton was capable of it:

> Thine are these mighty works, Parent of Good,
> Almighty, thine this everlasting frame.

But it seems to me that, after Milton, there is in literature less and less of that sort of invocation, even when there are many other sorts of inspiration. Shelley invented half a hundred goddesses, but he could not pray to them, not even as well as the old atheist Lucretius could pray to Venus, Mother of Rome. All Shelley's deities were abstractions; they were Beauty or Liberty or Love; but they might as well have been Algebra and Long Division, so far as inviting the gesture of worship goes. In this, as in everything else, what is the matter with the new pagan is that he is not a pagan; he has not any of the customs or consolations of a pagan. There is a little more of it, I admit, in the almost ironic invocations of Swinburne. But that is precisely because Swinburne was more deeply read, not in the new paganism, but in the old. He had at least gone into the temples of the old Greeks, even if it was to curse the gods as well as invoke them. But, on the whole, this gesture of invocation has rather gone out of poetry; and even our diabolists do not wave the wand with anything like a fine flourish, when they start to raise the devil.

IX. ON THE PLEASURES OF NO LONGER BEING VERY YOUNG

THERE are advantages in the advance through middle age into later life which are very seldom stated in a sensible way. Generally, they are stated in a sentimental way; in a general suggestion that all old men are equipped with beautiful snowy beards like Father Christmas and rejoice in unfathomable wisdom like Nestor. All this has caused the young people to be sceptical about the real advantages of the old people, and the true statement of those advantages sounds like a paradox. I would not say that old men grow wise, for men never grow wise; and many old men retain a very attractive childishness and cheerful innocence. Elderly people are often much more romantic than young people, and sometimes even more adventurous, having begun to realize how many things they do not know. It is a true proverb, no doubt, which says "There is no fool like an old fool." Perhaps there is no fool who is half so happy in his own fool's paradise. But, however this may be, it is true that the advantages of maturity are not those which are generally urged even in praise of it, and when they are truly urged they sound like an almost comic contradiction.

For instance, one pleasure attached to growing older is that many things seem to be growing younger; growing fresher and more lively than we once supposed them to be. We begin to see significance, or (in other words) to see life, in a large number of traditions, institutions, maxims, and codes of manners that seem in our first days to be dead. A young man grows up in a world that often seems to him intolerably old. He grows up among proverbs and precepts that appear to be quite stiff and senseless. He seems to be stuffed with stale things; to be given the stones of death instead of the bread of life; to be fed on the dust of the dead past; to live in a town of tombs. It is a very natural mistake, but it is a mistake. The advantage of advancing years lies in discovering that traditions are true, and therefore alive; indeed, a tradition is not even traditional except when it is alive. It is great fun to find out that the world has not repeated proverbs because they are proverbial, but because they are practical. Until I owned a dog, I never knew what is meant by the proverb about letting a sleeping dog lie, or the fable about the dog in the manger. Now those dead phrases are quite alive to me, for they are parts of a perfectly practical psychology. Until I went to live in the country, I had no notion of the meaning of the maxim, "It's an ill wind that blows nobody good." Now it seems to me as pertinent and even pungent as if it were a new remark just made to me by a neighbour at the garden gate. It is something to come to live in a world of living and significant things instead of dead and unmeaning things. And it is youth in revolt, even in righteous revolt, which sees its surroundings as dead and unmeaning. It is old age, and even second childhood, that has come to see that everything means something and that life itself has never died.

For instance, we have just seen a staggering turn of the wheel of fortune which has brought all the modern material pride and prosperity to a standstill. America, which a year or two ago seemed to have become one vast Eldorado studded with cities of gold, is almost as much embarrassed as England, and really much more embarrassed than Ireland. The industrial countries are actually finding it difficult to be industrial, while the old agricultural countries still find it possible to be industrious. Now, I do not pretend to have prophesied or expected this, for a man may cheerfully call a thing rotten without really expecting it to rot. But neither, certainly, did the young, the progressive, the prosperous, or the adventurous expect it. Yet all history and culture is stiff with proverbs and prophecies telling them to expect it.

The trouble is that they thought the proverbs and history a great deal too stiff. Again and again, with monotonous reiteration, both my young friends and myself had been told from childhood that fortune is fickle, that riches take to themselves wings and fly, that power can depart suddenly from the powerful, that pride goes before a fall, and insolence attracts the thunderbolt of the gods. But it was all unmeaning to us, and all the proverbs seemed stiff and stale, like dusty labels on neglected antiquities. We had heard of the fall of Wolsey, which was like the crash of a huge palace, still faintly rumbling through the ages; we had read of it in the words of Shakespeare, which possibly were not written by Shakespeare; we had learned them and learned nothing from them. We had read ten thousand times, to the point of tedium, of the difference between the Napoleon of Marengo and the Napoleon of Moscow; but we should never have expected Moscow if we had been looking at Marengo. We knew that Charles the Fifth resigned his crown, or that Charles the First lost his head; and we should have duly remarked "*Sic transit gloria mundi,*" after the incident, but not before it. We had been told that the Roman Empire declined, or that the Spanish Empire disintegrated; but no German ever really applied it to the German Empire, and no Briton to the British Empire. The very repetition of these truths will sound like the old interminable repetition of the truisms. And yet they are to me, at this moment, like amazing and startling discoveries, for I have lived to see the dead proverbs come alive.

This, like so many of the realizations of later life, is quite impossible to convey in words to anybody who has not reached it in this way. It is like a difference of dimension or plane, in which something which the young have long looked at, rather wearily, as a diagram has suddenly become a solid. It is like the indescribable transition from the inorganic to the organic; as if the stone snakes and birds of some ancient Egyptian inscription began to leap about like living things. The thing was a dead maxim when we were alive with youth. It becomes a living maxim when we are nearer to death. Even as we are dying, the whole world is coming to life.

Another paradox is this: that it is not the young people who realize the new world. The moderns do not realize modernity. They have never known anything else. They have stepped on to a moving platform which they hardly know to be moving, as a man cannot feel the daily movement of the earth. But he would feel it sharp enough if the earth suddenly moved the other way. The older generation consists of those who do remember a time when the world moved the other way. They do feel sharply and clearly the epoch which is beginning, for they were there before it began. It is one of the artistic advantages of the aged that they do see the new things relieved sharply against a background, their shape definite and distinct. To the young these new things are often themselves the background, and are hardly seen at all. Hence, even the most intelligent of innovators is often strangely mistaken about the nature of innovation and the things that are really new. And the Oldest Inhabitant will often indulge in a senile chuckle, as he listens to the Village Orator proclaiming that the village church will soon be swept away and replaced by a factory for chemicals. For the Oldest Inhabitant knows very well that nobody went to church in the days of his childhood except out of snobbishness, and that it is in his old age that the church has begun once more to be thronged with believers. In my capacity of Oldest Inhabitant (with senile chuckle), I will give one instance of a kindred kind. A man must be at least as old as I am in order to remember how utterly idiotic, inconceivable, and crazily incredible it once seemed that any educated or even reasonably shrewd person should confess that he believed in *ghosts*. You must be nearly the Oldest Inhabitant to know with what solid scorn and certainty the squire and the parson denied the possibility of the village ghost; the parson even more emphatically than the squire. The village ghost was instantly traced to the village drunkard or the village liar. Educated people *knew* that the dead do not return in the world of sense. Those who remember those times, and have lived to see a man of science like Sir Oliver Lodge founding quite a fashionable religion, are amused to hear a young man say the world is moving away from the supernatural. They know in what direction it has really moved.

X. ON MR. MENCKEN AND FUNDAMENTALISM

It is the custom to make fun of Fundamentalism and to suggest that American religion is rather antiquated. But I sometimes think that American irreligion is much more antiquated than American religion, and that the sceptic can be more of a fossil than the sectarian. Both, of course, are sects only representing sections. America contains many other brighter and better things; and certainly America is sufficiently advanced and adventurous, especially in certain forms of scientific practice, to balance anything belated in certain forms of scientific theory. But the belated forms exist, and seem to be still under the illusion that they are advanced forms. There seem still to be places in the world where the earth shakes if the indomitable Darrow mentions the unmentionable Darwin. I am not sure that they may not be referring to Erasmus Darwin.

Mr. H. L. Mencken is at least a brilliant man of letters and ought to know better. But he, I gather, has just been coming out in defence of the dead and buried negations of the nineteenth century, and gallantly doing his best to prevent American science from moving with the times. His way of doing it seems to be to play about with the word "Scientist" in opposition to some other word like the word "Physicist." "Scientist" is a horrible word to be driven to use, though I have often been driven to use it; but all these terms for the study of science are in a very unscientific confusion. It would be embarrassing to summon a physician and be visited by a physicist. Yet on the parallel of physics and metaphysics, the former word would seem more logical. Few of us have ever, in desperate haste, summoned a metaphysician. But it would be far more frightful and terrifying to be visited by a metaphysicist. Subject to the further clarification of the language, I presume Mr. Mencken to mean by a scientist either a man who specializes in all sciences (a somewhat alarming figure) or else a man who really specializes in one science in a scientific way. Mr. Mencken chooses to contradict flatly the principal living physicists, who have studied physics in a strictly scientific way. I do not know if he has studied the science in any way, but I am pretty sure that he has not studied it in that way. When, therefore, he says of the distinguished men whose close study of matter has not led them to materialism, that it only shows that they can be physicists without being scientists, it throws a yet more uncanny light on that very ugly word.

Apparently a scientist is a man who surveys all the sciences, without any particular study of them, and then gives expression to his own moral principles or prejudices. In this way it is proved that Mr. Mencken is a scientist. I also am a scientist; but in my time it used to be called a journalist.

It is great fun, for what it really means is that the scientific materialist never cared for science but only for materialism. So long as he supposed that material inquiry supported materialism, he roared and bellowed at us that we must "accept the conclusions of science." But he is not the least inclined himself to accept the conclusions of science, if they happen to go against his own crude and clumsy creed. The Darwinians would have been hysterical with horror if any Victorian journalist had told them that Darwin might be a biologist without being a scientist. Twenty years ago, it would have been atrociously antiquated to say that Haeckel was not really a scientist, though it is now much less clear that he was a scientist than that he was a monist. He was, anyhow, a propagandist, and a pretty unscrupulous propagandist; but we were all supposed to swallow what he said at once, because he was Science. The new physicists are not propagandists, but Mr. Mencken, so far from reverencing them as Science, desperately refuses to respect them even as scientists. And he takes up this extraordinary position for no reason in the world, except that they will not say exactly what he tells them to say, in the world of morals and metaphysics. But it is rather hard to ask them to drop all their scientific work for fear they should get a little ahead of Mr. Mencken.

God forbid that I should blame Mr. Mencken for being a Diehard and dying in the last ditch, even in the rather muddy ditch of a dead materialism. If he still thinks the old-fashioned science was right, he is perfectly right to be old-fashioned. But he will hardly expect us not to laugh at him, when we consider how we were derided as Diehards for being ready to die in a ditch which we thought more deep and rather less dirty. He is now, apparently, in exactly the same situation as we were, except that our principle has satisfied the intelligence of teeming populations for two thousand years, while his prejudice has broken down as soon as it was set up. So far as the teeming populations are concerned, it has ended before it had begun. For modern monism and materialism were never accepted by simple people, and are now being abandoned by scientific people. To be true to them when they lie under such a complication of disasters and disillusions may be admired as chivalric in the sense of quixotic; but Mr. Mencken would be the first to insist that it is allowable to smile at Don Quixote.

I have so warm an admiration for Mr. Mencken as the critic of Puritan pride and stupidity that I regret that he should thus try to make himself out a back number out of mere irreligious irritation. He has been the hammer of those false idealists who call themselves moral because they demand the Prohibition of a few hard drinks, and dare not say a word of the Prohibition of hard dealings, of hard bargains that break the poor, and the brutal ethics tolerated in business. I sympathize so much with this that I do not mind the hammer being flourished sometimes a little cheaply and ostentatiously, like an auctioneer's hammer; nor do I demand in the present case that it should tap as cautiously and scientifically as a geological hammer. But I do demand that it should go somewhere near hitting the right nail on the head, even if it be hit with all the windy violence of some Nietzschean imitation of the Hammer of Thor. I do not mind Mr. Mencken being destructive, like his master Nietzsche before him. What I complain of here is that he is not destructive enough. He not only dare not destroy, but he cannot even bear to watch the destruction of a few blunders and blind dogmas of old Victorian science. The Fundamentalists are funny enough, and the funniest thing about them is their name. For, whatever else the Fundamentalist is, he is not fundamental. He is content with the bare letter of Scripture—the translation of a translation, coming down to him by the tradition of a tradition—without venturing to ask for its original authority. But Mr. Mencken, in his latest phase, is almost as superficial as a Fundamentalist. I should have expected a man of his intelligence to be something fundamental, if it were only a fundamental sceptic. But a real fundamental sceptic, as he has existed in Hellas or in India, or possibly in the cavern of Zarathustra, would never be frightened because the new scientific study of matter leads to mathematical abstractions and abysses. He would never be alarmed because the world now revealed by the physicists is not even physical. It is the business of the agnostic to admit that he knows nothing; and he might the more gracefully admit it touching sciences about which he knows precious little. As it is, it seems as if the agnostic were transformed into the atheist, and a pretty stale and provincial sort of atheist; what might be called respectfully the village atheist. Even then, I suspect that I should sympathize with him in practice, in his free fight with the village

Puritans in front of the village inn. But, just as I should prefer him to admit that even the village chemist knows something about chemistry, or the village physician about physic, I would suggest that even physicists do know something about physics.

XI. ON ANTHONY TROLLOPE: HISTORIAN

I WAS recently reading an article on Anthony Trollope, one of the many that have appeared in literary magazines since critics have discovered that his work can be treated as literature, when they used only to treat it as fiction. He is a rather rare example of a man who has been taken more seriously after his death than in his presence. The Victorians tended to regard Trollope as light literature, and Thackeray and even Dickens as more serious literature. The modern critics, rightly or wrongly, are disposed to treat Trollope more seriously, and even Dickens and Thackeray more lightly. Of course, Trollope is treated in both fashions, according to the taste of the critic. Mr. Hugh Walpole has cultivated the Trollope style both by precept and example; and Father Ronald Knox has made a most elaborate and detailed map of Barsetshire, and annotated it with stern queries about why Dr. Thorne took so long to get to Plumstead Episcopi, or what Mr. Gresham was doing on the wrong road to Framley Parsonage. These are not the right examples; for I, alas! have not the powerful detective and documentary brain of Father Knox.

But it is broadly true that Trollope has again attracted many people from many aspects. And yet there is one aspect of Trollope which I think has been entirely neglected, and which I think is of very great and vital importance to the history of England.

The critic in question says of Trollope, truly enough in the main: "He scarcely concerned himself with the lower orders." We may add that the whole system of English squirearchy scarcely concerned itself with the lower orders; or only in the same vague and well-meaning way as Trollope. But when the critic adds, "His values were those of the middle class," he misses the point—the point which I think important about English history. It is not really true, as a whole, that his characters were middle class. It might be said more truly that Dickens dealt largely with the middle class, though doubtless more largely with the lower middle class, and even the lower class. But Trollope really deals with the upper middle class in so far as it is attached to the upper class. Squire Gresham was not middle class; and I fancy that Archdeacon Grantly would have been very much surprised to be told he was. I draw a veil over the fury of Mrs. Proudie, who would probably, I admit, have been even more indignant at the description if it happened to be true. Dr. Thorne was, in the ordinary sense, of the professional middle class; but we are never allowed to forget that his family was older and prouder than the De Courcys. Most of the Government clerks are of the more or less aristocratic class from which Government clerks were, and to some extent still are, chiefly drawn. In other words, we shall not learn the first historical lesson from Trollope till we realize that he bears witness to England as an aristocratic State; and not, as our friends the Communists would say, as a *bourgeois* State. But there is a further development of this historical truth, which I think rather curious. Trollope bears witness to a big historical fact about our past, and does it all the more solidly and sincerely because he has no notion that he is doing it at all.

I know it was the fashion in the Victorian times to say that England was represented by its Great Middle Class and not by its aristocracy. That was the artfulness of its aristocracy. Never did a governing class govern so completely, by saying it did not govern at all. The middle-class Englishman was always pushed into the foreground; while the rulers remained in the background. It was the middle-class Englishman who wrote letters to *The Times;* it was not he who informed *The Times*. It was the middle-class man who went to the political meeting; it was not he who sent down the candidate. The governing class governed by the perfectly simple principle of keeping all the important things to themselves; and giving the papers and the public unimportant things to discuss. When Earl Balfour (one of the last great survivals of the governing class) said languidly that he never read the newspapers, everybody laughed, as if he had said that he could not read the alphabet. In fact, of course, he never read the newspapers because he had read the State papers. Why should he read all the nonsense that was served out to the public when he knew all the real secrets which were kept as secrets of State?

But when we have realized that the England of Trollope was still an aristocratic England, there is a further distinction, which Trollope never notices, but always makes clear. His evidence is alone enough to upset Macaulay and Green and the whole Whig theory of our history taught in the schools. The really interesting fact to be inferred from Trollope is this. Nineteenth-century England is *not* a country in which we have a populace led by a Liberal middle class on one side and a powerful Tory nobility led by Dukes and Earls on the other. The division of the parties is totally different, and unconsciously betrays the real secret, not only of the nineteenth, but of the eighteenth and seventeenth centuries. It betrays the truth about the Glorious Revolution of 1688, and the nature of the new system which it really introduced. The Crown did not pass from James II to William III. Like many stolen treasures, it was cut up: it was cut up into coronets.

Let anybody, reading Trollope carefully, note what the real division between the parties was. There is a large proportion of minor gentry, who may be called middle class, if we will, who are certainly numerous and not very rich: doctors, parsons, small squires, and yeomen and all sorts of plain and hard-working people. Now *these* people are all Tories. They inherit the old Tory tradition of loyalty to a king, which belonged to purely middle-class people like Dr. Johnson or Dr. Goldsmith. Far above all these people, like gods on Olympus, like higher beings living on a loftier plane, there are two or three people who are of prodigious public importance, like emperors or kings. The tone of everybody else in talking about them implies the remote condescension of a sovereign. The obvious example is the Duke of Omnium. He is spoken of as playing a great princely part like a prince. We need not deny him the credit, but we need not disguise the fact that his importance rested on being what we call a millionaire. More presentable, I admit, than the millionaires who are flattered to-day. But he is ruler of all England because he is gigantically rich. Now *this* kind of man is always a

Whig.

What the serious historians have disguised the frivolous novelist has detected. Their histories are fiction and his fiction is history. That is the truth; and that is Trollope's unconscious witness to what the Whigs really did in English history; why they were able to overthrow the Stuarts; why they were able to dominate the common traditional Tories like Dr. Thorne. What the Revolution did was obviously not to establish a democracy; not even to establish a normal and national gentry; not even to establish a mere rustic squirearchy. It was to establish certain great magnates, whose wealth and power was far out of proportion to that of the ordinary gentleman, let alone the ordinary citizen. They owned everything and Trollope knew it. What other possible meaning is there in the title of *The Duke of Omnium*? Thackeray also knew it. What possible other meaning is there in that fine satiric flourish, "I am not a Whig . . . but oh, how I should like to be!"? Even the waiters and couriers on the Continent knew it. What other meaning was in the Arabian Nights legend of the English Milord? Everybody seems to have known it, except the people who taught history in the schools and universities of England.

XII. ON THE WAY OF THE WORLD

It was Matthew Arnold, if I remember right, who invented or popularized the phrase "the way the world is going," a motto for social reformers only too easily adapted into a motto for snobs. It is not really even a simple, let alone a safe, guide; as can be easily tested in his own case. After all, if it comes to that, what way *was* the world going in the time of Matthew Arnold? We are far enough from it to look back to it, and, when we look back to it, the world seems to be going all ways at once. It was certainly a time when the Philistines, as he called them, the middle-class mercantile Liberals of the school of Cobden and Bright, were still marching from victory to victory. And yet the end of the Liberal century was crowned, or crushed, by the Jingo journalism of the Kipling epoch, with War, Imperialism, and everything that the old Liberals loathed. In one sense the world was more sceptical and scientific; in every sense it seemed more sceptical and scientific; and yet the mystical and religious reaction increased steadily from then till now. In short, when we look back on that time we see not a tide but an eddy, or a welter of eddies, in which each person is paddling his own canoe desperately in his own direction. Arnold wanted to go back to Athens; Newman to go back to Rome; Carlyle to go back to Scandinavia; Schopenhauer to go back to India; Nietzsche to go back to chaos. I do not say there was no predominant influence among these influences, but I do say that it was not so simple as Arnold and some other people thought it; and, so far from simplifying itself with distance, it seems with distance to grow more dizzy and distracted. Wherever that age was drifting, it was to the place where we are now. And where in the world are we?

There is one case of this complexity that always amuses me: the way in which the abstract assumptions of an age are often contradicted by its concrete customs and amusements. The superficial examples are obvious enough. In theory this is the age of Prohibition; in practice it is the age of Cocktails. In theory women are working in the world on an assumption of absolute equality with men. In practice vast numbers are reading the novels of Miss Ethel M. Dell and all sorts of rubbishy tales and essays about the fascination of sheikhs and cavemen. In theory the State has been practically secularized and theology is a dead and threadbare thing, dismissed disdainfully in every other paragraph as a lumber of "creeds and dogmas." In practice no newspaper can apparently pay its way without plastering itself all over with headlines and captions about the position of Christianity, the nature of Christ, the immortality of the soul, the future of the Churches, and a whole picture-gallery of portraits of popular clergymen. But there is one particular contradiction which I would note here, between the tone of such religious journalism and something else that might rather be called spiritual literature. At a moment when the popular religion, or at least the religion preached in the popular press, all points one way, the work of the most modern and independent artists points the other. The newspapers are all God and no devil. The novels are all devils and no God.

The tone of that religious journalism, or whatever we call it, is something that people call Optimism. It is a bad word, but it can sometimes stand for a good thing. I have used it myself in other days, merely in opposition to Pessimism, and as meaning the primary conviction that life is worth living and the world is worthy of our efforts for it. But nowadays it means something much more; or, rather, something immeasurably less. It means a sort of cheap cheeriness, at the back of which there is a curious sort of hollow unbelief in reality. Men boasted of being Optimists about the war; which is like being Optimists about the weather. A man may try to be cheerful even if there is a thunderstorm; but these lunatics talked as if they could prevent a thunderstorm by being cheerful. Those who propose to be cheerful when struck by lightning introduce a more mystical question. So people now boast of being Optimists about Trade; this is more vulgar but less irrational, precisely because trade is a less real thing than war. Some are surprised that the same American civilization should produce Christian Science and commercial salesmanship. But in fact Christian Science is very like commercial salesmanship. Both rest on the idea that facts can be conjured away by moods and mesmerism. The perfect Scientist persuades a man that he hasn't got what he has got. The perfect Salesman persuades a man that he does want what he doesn't want. We may call it, in a complimentary phrase, the power of spirit over matter. We may call it, in a less complimentary phrase, the power of lies over facts. But this spirit of persuasion, or illusion, does pervade our time in good and bad forms, and especially in one popular religious form. I have remarked before that Spiritualism, for instance, while it does not affirm that all Spirits are good, does rather tend to ignore the suggestion that some are bad. And it will be agreed that the general tone of all the True Christianity and New Religions that pervades the newspapers rather leaves out the possibility that anything is bad. One would infer from these lay sermons that there is no difficulty about being happy, if it be only accompanied by being hazy. Some of the writers deal with the tremendous and pulverizing paradox of the Love of God, especially in the aspect of faith in the God of Love, as if it were not only perfectly self-evident, but as if it could have no effect except to make us self-satisfied. The thunderous riddle of the *"Est Deus Caritatis"* which broke above the dying Brand after his life of agony on the peak of his perfect renunciation, seems to be uttered chirpily every morning to every clerk or stockbroker who will be sufficiently broadminded to play golf instead of going to church. Carlyle complained of people who were at ease in Zion. But the new Zionism thinks it enough to prove that it is easier still not to be in Zion at all. Whatever else it does encourage, the dread of devilry or definite evil is admittedly a thing that it does not encourage. We could read reams and files of the new newspaper theology and not find even a mention of that fear of demons that was felt by all our fathers.

Very well; that is the way the world is supposed to have gone in our time. But when we read the literature of our time, especially when it is really literary, we find something quite the contrary. The most distinguished men of letters, the novelists or the new poets, often have no more definite beliefs than the newspaper believers. They are quite as pure from the taint of creed, dogma, or intellectually intelligible statement of faith. Most of them are probably agnostics; and in that sense do not believe in God, let alone the devil. And yet they are perpetually writing about devils. They are always at it. Book after book comes out, of which the theme is some strange psychological wickedness, encouraged more or less by some more strange psychical influence. One distinguished novelist writes a book about Pan, as a positive influence and a highly unpleasant influence, fully worthy of his ancient association with Panic. Another distinguished novelist devotes another imaginative novel to a dark and terrible deity of the South Americans, worshipped in former ages with torture and blood. Among the masterpieces of the last twenty or thirty years, those that stand out in my own memory with startling power are almost all of them stories of necromancy or diabolic possession, often written by men who had no definite religious affiliations, but who had imagination carrying all the solidity of conviction. I look back over the whole of that long period, that has been littered to the sky with newspaper philosophies preaching cheerfulness and optimism, and ignorance of evil. And the two things that stand out in my memory for their solidity and sincerity and power, staring like stone gargoyles of gigantic stature, are both things that seem to face the other way from the whole recent movement of the world. I remember the real literary thrill which I felt long ago when reading *The Turn of the Screw,* and how it woke within me again long after, under the suffocating vividness of *Seaton's Aunt.*

XIII. ON THE NEW INSULARITY

THAT a heresy is a half-truth is a very old and familiar example of a whole truth; but a truth that is not often realized as a whole. Most mistaken people mean well, and all mistaken people mean something. There is something to be said for every error, but, whatever may be said for it, the most important thing to be said about it is that it is erroneous. On the principle that half a loaf is better than no bread, it ought to be true that half a truth is better than no verity. But in practice, it is not so much a case of the half loaf of the proverb as of the half apple of the fairy-tale; the apple of which one half was poisoned by the wicked stepmother for the good princess. At least, as modern mental feeding goes, to stop in the middle of the meal is often to eat the poison without eating the antidote. And if we look back on history, we shall see it largely encumbered and crushed with half-truths; we shall wonder how it happened so often that a whole age or generation was content with a half-truth, without making the faintest effort to find the other half. We shall wonder how one fashion could be entirely set upon fame or glory, or another upon order and symmetry, or another upon discovery and adventure; and be unable to understand how men could sacrifice all other things to each of these things in turn. It may be that we shall never fully understand why our fathers did it, for we certainly do not in the least understand why we do it ourselves.

There are certain half-truths that are even now allowed to occupy the whole mind. There are certain statements that are true as far as they go, and even important and interesting as far as they go, which are yet incessantly being used to stop the mind from going any farther. One of these, for example, is the phrase we find in the phraseology of all our literature and journalism; "Rapid modern communications are bringing different parts of the world nearer and nearer together. It takes but a few days to go to Siberia by train; it may take but a few hours to go there by aeroplane. Instead of being at the ends of the earth, Siberia may yet be a sort of suburb like Surbiton." But nobody stops to ask himself whether Siberia really is like Surbiton; in what respect it is really unlike Surbiton, or, above all, whether it is not in some respects growing more unlike Surbiton. For another process is going on, parallel to the process of the connexion of routes, and it is the disconnexion of ideas. Suppose, for the sake of argument, that some bold and romantic adventurer from Surbiton had gone to Siberia a hundred years ago. Doubtless he would have found the people there something like savages; perhaps, to his too refined suburban eye, something hardly different from the beasts of the field. And yet, without claiming any antiquarian scholarship about that somewhat obscure district, I would undertake to say that there were some ideas common to the Siberian and the Suburban. I should guess, for instance, that the Asiatic savages had some rudimentary idea of private property. I suspect that Siberian would have said, "This is my spear," as confidently as the Surbitonian would have said, "This is my umbrella." It is probable that there was some sort of religion in Siberia, as it is probable that there is some sort of religion in Surbiton. The traveller to-day could get ten times more quickly to the Siberian village than he could have got there a hundred ago. But it is no longer so absolutely certain that he would find these simple things if he got there. He might find it was already a Communist village, not in the old and normal sense of a communal village; but in the fixed fanatical sense of a Bolshevist village. He might find the villagers being dogmatically taught the doctrine of Bolshevism; taught that it is really wicked to own an umbrella or still more wicked to wield a spear. He might find, for almost the first time in human history, a people being systematically instructed in the theory that there is neither God nor gods. That means that the village, which is geographically so much nearer, is now philosophically much farther away. And this is due to a new division in the thoughts of man; to the rise of a new sect and the separation of a whole civilization from the general human tradition. There are many modern examples of the disproportionate size of such queer modern sects; there is the rather comic example of Prohibition. It is only a half-truth to say that America comes nearer and nearer to Europe, as ships fly faster and faster across the Atlantic. A ship took heaven knows how long to get from England to America in the days of the American Revolution and the Fathers of the Republic. But the traveller in the ship found Washington drinking wine in his house in Virginia, exactly as he had left Lord North drinking wine in his house in London. If you had told them that it was wicked to drink wine, Washington would have stared just as North would have stared at such a statement. A Moslem morality had not then arisen beyond the Atlantic, to divide America from Christendom. Wine was thicker than water. It united men of a common culture; and the English race on either side of the ocean was only divided by liquid and not by liquor.

For that matter, our own British politics have

lately illustrated vividly enough the fact that a division accompanies such a unification. We have seen it, first in the case of Ireland and then in the case of India. It was exactly at the time when they were easiest to reach that they were hardest to hold. No improvement in the trains from Euston or the boats from Holyhead, can alter the fact that our folly allowed Ireland to float farther and farther away, in the sea of the spirit, till it was as remote as a South Sea Island. It was perhaps too much to expect that we should ever really understand India; but in the old days it was at least understood how much we proposed to understand. If a hostile critic likes to put it so, it was understood that we should continue to misunderstand. But at least something was understood; and in the present welter and dissolution of bonds, it is not too much to say that nothing is understood. The new India is more of a riddle than the old; and the country grows more mysterious as it grows more near, or even more new. For we are for the first time near enough to feel the full force of the differences; and that sort of silent shock of collision is occurring with the closer communications all over the world. But there is, moreover, as I have said, a moral division due to the growth of new ideas. When we dealt with the active resistance of Hyder Ali the Moslem, both sides were fighting with the same weapons and in the same world. When we deal with the passive resistance of Gandhi the Mahatma, we are in a world as unfamiliar as magic.

The paradox of this parallel of contraction and expansion is really simple enough. It follows on the modern attempt to combine wild spiritual speculation with systematic scientific order. Philosophy sprouts and sprawls in every direction, and science tries in vain to tie the bundle together. Men were united by religions and loyalties, and then it did not matter how widely they were scattered. A clan or tribe would be spread thinly over a whole moorland or prairie. Each hut would be as solitary as a hermitage, but they would be hermits of the same creed. The modern method is to stick up a row of villas all exactly alike, and all close together for convenience of electricity and drainage. But the man living in the first house may be a Buddhist, and in the second a Papist, and in the third an atheist, and in the fourth a diabolist; and each villa is an isolated universe.

XIV. ON CHRISTIAN SCIENCE

THE friends of Christian Science say proudly that very good business men are Christian Scientists. The foes of Christian Science say, unkindly, that Christian Scientists are very good business men. I will not debate whether these are only two ways of saying the same thing, far less whether it is a nice thing to say. The former point radiantly to rows and rows of hard-headed millionaires, reverently listening to readings from *Science and Health,* under the rather extraordinary impression that the presence of millionaires helps them to prove that Christian Science is Christian. The latter explain that Mrs. Eddy, though doubtless unconscious of the existence of matter, was not wholly unconscious of the existence of money. I have no intention of entering upon these purely personal feuds here. But I should like to point out that there really is a moral connexion between the two things, that extends beyond the defined boundaries of either. Just as there are more invisible (and therefore, presumably, more spiritual) forms of money than mere material coin—such as dues, debts, expectations, dead men's shoes, mortgage, usury, economic threats and blackmail, and all the other purer and more immaterial forms of wealth—so there are indirect and impalpable influences of Christian Science which affect many who do not profess to be Scientists and could not, without some implication of humour, pretend to be Christians.

The truth is that in one sense Christian Science has succeeded and really become the religion of the age, though it does not follow of necessity that this is a compliment to the age. I do not mean by this that most people have studied and accepted Mrs. Eddy's original metaphysics; if, indeed, they were original, or if they were really Mrs. Eddy's. Still less do I mean that the world accepts the original morals of Christian Science, for I am told that they are no longer accepted even by Christian Scientists. The primary principle of the cult obviously forbade them to run for a doctor if Mrs. Eddy broke her leg, since either the leg, or certainly the break, or possibly both, were illusions of Mortal Mind. Whether there really were people who would have let a man bleed to death, because the blood was a result of the mere flow of his thoughts, I have my doubts; but that did seem to be involved in some of the original definitions, though not, I understand, in some of the later modifications of them. But this practical morality about doctors does not here concern me, however practical or unpractical it may be. What I mean, when I say that this is the age of Christian Science, is not that most people living in it are in any sense Christian Scientists. I mean that the world is in a certain mood, of which Christian Science is the expression and exaggeration. It is not so much that the age could not find a more accommodating religion, as that the religion could not find a more accommodating age. Men have sometimes talked about people who were Christians before Christ, and in one sense there were certainly any number of people who were Christian Scientists before Christian Science. There was something in the whole air and movement of that time, and especially of that nation, and it was of a curious blind, sweeping, and abnormal sort. The air was rather like a whirlwind and the movement rather like a whirlpool. It had an element of formlessness that was rather that of abstraction than anarchy; that rushed headlong, yet followed the curves of a tendency or a fate. Indeed, among the queer jokes so often to be found in American names, there is none more quaintly expressive than the very name of Mrs. Eddy.

The truth about the tendency was this: that the world had become a world of Commerce. And there is about Commerce an invisible thing that may be called Confidence; even if it sometimes means no more than the Confidence Trick. It depends on faith, even if it prove to be bad faith. It does *not* depend on plain matters of material fact and experience. The millionaires in the Church of Christ Scientist are supposed to be hard-headed; I have myself a suspicion that they are rather soft-headed. But, anyhow, they do not really deal in hardware; they do emphatically deal in what may be called soft goods. They deal in things that easily receive impressions from without, and are especially sensitive to the impressions that we call depressions. They deal in rumours, in understandings, in fictitious values, in temporary offers, in things that are never what they seem, and seldom do exactly what they promise. Business is such stuff as dreams are made on, and its little life is rounded with a slump.

This nervous and not very sane state of affairs is the origin of Optimism and the general advice to the salesman to Keep Smiling. If he left off smiling for one single second, he might blight the market for hundreds of miles around. The whole condition has now become so terribly atmospheric; not in the milder sense of men suffering from the atmosphere, but in the almost agonizing sense of men making the atmosphere. That is why the whole of this commercial world is struck by the stubborn dissatisfaction or harsh discontent of the more rooted rural populations. They say that the farmer always grumbles; and so he does, for he can afford to grumble. He thinks the weather is bad, but he knows that his grumbling will not make it worse. He knows he cannot produce a cloud in the sky by every curse that comes to his tongue; that he cannot blight his own crops, even by declaring falsely that they are blighted. He cannot create a slump in turnips merely by turning a melancholy face upon them, or frown at the cabbages until they close weak and quiet when they began brisk and strong. He is dealing with absolute and unalterable realities, and, as he is dealing with real facts, he can express his real feelings. He is, in a rather curious and eccentric sense, in a position in which the truth has made him free. He is a realist because he is dealing with realities. The commercial man almost has to be a romanticist because he so often deals with unrealities. And that is what Americans mean when they talk about The Romance of Salesmanship.

Now, for an atmosphere so atmospheric as that the obvious religion was Christian Science, with its general suggestion of men creating their own atmosphere. To say that there was no such thing as a headache was part of the same mentality as saying that there would be no such thing as a slump; it was of the very essence of that mythology and genealogy that the wish was father of the thought. It had all kinds of minor manifestations, apart from any acceptance of that particular creed; but it was obviously more in touch with that particular creed than with any other creed. It was closely akin to all that astonishing mass of advertisement and suggestion about Personality and Will-Power and all the rest which we see sprawling over so many American books and magazines. It is an ironic jest that the religion is revealed, or betrayed, by its images or icons. The American papers show portraits of men who have Personality; which is why they all look exactly alike.

I have remarked recently that the world is now occupied with the Study of the Mind rather than with the Use of the Mind. This is what is meant by calling it the Age of Psychology. It is also what is meant by calling it, in a somewhat sinister sense, the Age of Physical Jerks. It is a nervous and unrestful sort of optimism that is thus perpetually trying to impose a mood upon the objective universe, and the world, like Wall Street, is liable to reactions of panic. But certainly Christian Science did for a time suit the mood, if it does not for any long period suit the mind; if, indeed, we return to using the mind instead of merely doctoring it with drugs.

XV. ON REST CURES FOR NATIONS

We certainly need a new theory of Progress, for all existing theories about the future have a very hopeless air of being things of the past. There is even a detachable grain of truth in the doctrine of Spengler, which roughly maintains that there is no such thing as Progress, but only Progresses. That is, there is such a thing as one civilization becoming completely civilized in its own way, and then getting out of the way to make room for a totally different civilization. Unfortunately, every heathen seems fated to be a fatalist, and every fatalist seems fated to be a pessimist. The heathen in his blindness bows down to wood and stone; in other words, he is pitifully cramped and crushed by the study of botany and geology. Sometimes he even passes from botany to biology, or, worse still, to anthropology. Now, in these dead or undeveloped things, it is more or less true that there is no Progress, but only Progresses. It is not easy to compare one completed phase with another; it is idle to ask whether old red sandstone is redder than greengages are green. The fossil that was and the flower that is cannot call to each other across the ages, and though there may be, in one sense, an upward spirit of evolution, it is not a spiritual spiral, or, as the Yankees would say, a live wire. There is not, in that manifest manner, at least, a memory in nature; but there is a memory of mankind. Cultures do not so completely perish as the pessimists pretend. Men do own the cave-drawings of a Neolithic man, as birds do not own the fossil of a pterodactyl. Still, there is a truth in that substitution of Progresses for Progress.

The truth seems to me to be this: that men do from time to time make special efforts; these are often crowned with success, and when they are crowned with success they generally end in failure. But that leaves on one side the question of the ordinary human life, which existed before the effort and still exists after the effort. Rome made a great effort and civilized a great part of the world, and the effort was followed by the Dark Ages. But the Dark Ages were not sub-human, any more than the Roman Empire was superhuman. It has been said by historical scholars that the simplicity of the Dark Ages refreshed the world like a sleep. It is certainly true that nations can be notably vigorous and hopeful at the end of what is called a period of decline and might more properly be called a period of neglect. Spain is far more vigorous and hopeful at this moment than many parts of the vast industrial field of what are considered successful societies. Spain made a great effort in the sixteenth century, and opened a new world of wealth and discovery; then it began to sink slowly out of sight. But Spaniards were not stupid and stunted savages in the time of Goya any more than in the time of Velasquez. Very likely the time will soon come when the Spaniards will make another effort; and for this purpose it is likely enough that their repose or retirement will have left them healthier and happier than most other people. In fact, we need a new theory or conception in history; the conception of the historical holiday. Perhaps the Dark Ages were a holiday, if they were a little like a dull and rainy holiday. But there is something to be said for a vacation, even in the literal sense of a vacuum. Anyhow, I think it extremely probable that the Spaniards will turn up again as fresh as paint, even the paint of Velasquez. They have not been so much exhausted and depressed by our dismal industrial materialism or our vast capitalist responsibilities. They have been refreshed and rejuvenated by a little decay; and have thoroughly enjoyed themselves for three centuries as a dying nation.

I would not insist everywhere on substituting, for the respectable old theory of the Revolution, this disturbing and dangerous theory of the Rest Cure. No doubt it might be overdone. People might go on decaying a little too long, and degenerate more than was really good for their health. I propose only a moderate indulgence in ruin; a cautious and temperate use of a return to barbarism. There are many quite modern people in whom the merest touch of decomposition, the merest soupçon of corruption and rottenness, would be enough to reassure me. But there are some modern people who are a great deal too modern; who are quite certainly devouring and destroying themselves with the nonsense of novelty, and trying always to hear of something later than the very latest. They are visibly growing old in order to keep up with their youth. They are wasting away to nothing, for want of a little nothing to do. If only some of their friends would persuade them to go away for a few centuries of superstition and ignorance, like the people of the Dark Ages, they might come back and astonish the world by something that the world had never seen before, like Gothic architecture or the portraits in the *Canterbury Tales*.

Anyhow, there is something to be said for this theory of the periodical enterprise of humanity. One advantage of it is that it resettles in a sane proportion all that question which was discussed in an earlier article: the question of the real case for the Noble Savage and Rousseau's conception of a return to Nature. So long as scientific men merely despised savages (much more than the missionaries who were charged with despising them), the case seemed simple enough. If primitive people were always more cruel and vindictive, as well as more clumsy and ignorant, than we are, then it was possible to present a progressive humanity, which every day and in every way was growing better and better. But (as I remarked elsewhere) even the story of simple tribes is not so simple. There is evidence of simple tribes that are actually milder in their punishments than we are, or kinder to their children than we are; or at least than we very recently were. But though this upsets the whole progressive theory that we civilized people are better than the savages in all respects, it does not force us to the contrary conclusion that the savages are better than we are in all respects. It is arguable that when men marched out on a special enterprise, they had to adopt a special discipline. Civilization might in some ways have more severe laws, because it had more serious problems. There might be harder lessons to learn, because there was more to be learned. The progressive tribe might be under martial law, while the conservative tribe was under common law. But the former might none the less be marching to the promised land.

For instance, there is a tiresome journalistic habit of fulsomely praising ourselves, and fatuously despising our fathers, because we no longer hang a man for forgery. But, as a fact, it was not an early primitive habit, but a late progressive habit, to hang a man for forgery. The law punishing forgery with death appeared quite late in our history, and was a result of our advancing civilization. It was a highly modern sort of thing to do. For forgery did not become frightfully important until finance and commercial contracts, and banking business of all sorts, had become important. I am very glad that men are no longer hanged for forgery. But I can quite imagine a simple and artless tribe of savages among whom the habit of imitating another man's handwriting would appear as gay and innocent as making faces in imitation of another man's face. If Hiawatha wrote his name in picture-writing on the smooth bark of the birch-tree, there would be no particular harm in Chibiabos playfully copying his friend's particular way of drawing a wigwam or a rising sun. No; there is something after all in the Noble Savage; there is something at least in the Happy Savage. But that does not prove that the tribe should not sacrifice some of its happiness when the Great Spirit bids it go forth to war.

XVI. ON PHILOSOPHY *VERSUS* FICTION

LOOKING back on a wild and wasted life, I realize that I have especially sinned in neglecting to read novels. I mean the really novel novels; for such old lumber as Dickens and Jane Austen I know fairly well. If instead of trifling away my time over pamphlets about Collectivism or Co-operation, plunging for mere pleasure into the unhealthy excitement of theological debates with dons, or enjoying the empty mirth of statistics about Poland and Czechoslovakia, I had quietly sat at home doing my duty and reading every novel as it comes out, I might be a more serious and earnest man than I am to-day. If instead of loitering to laugh over something, merely because it happened to be laughable, I had walked stiffly and sternly on to the Circulating Library, and put myself under the tuition of our more passionate lady novelists, I might by this time be as intense as they. If instead of leading a riotous life, scrapping with Mr. Shaw about Socialism, or Dean Inge about Science, I had believed everything I was told about marriage by an unmarried young woman in an avowedly imaginary story, I might now have a more undisturbed faith and simplicity. Novels are the great monument of the amazing credulity of the modern mind; for people believe them quite seriously even though they do not pretend to be true.

But it is really true, alas! that I have failed to follow adequately the development of serious fiction. I do not admit that I have entirely failed to follow the development of serious facts. Not only have I discussed Labour with Socialists, or Science with Scientists, but I have argued with myself about other things, so new and true that I cannot get anybody else to argue about them. The world-wide power of trusts, for instance, is a thing that is never attacked and never defended. It seems to have been completed without ever having been proposed; we might say without ever having been begun. The small shopkeeper has been destroyed in the twentieth century, as the small yeoman was destroyed in the eighteenth century. But for the yeoman there was protest and regret; great poets sang his dirge, and great orators like Cobbett died trying to avenge his death. But the modern destructive changes seem to be too new to be noticed. Perhaps they are too enormous to be seen. No; I do not think it can be fairly said that I have neglected the most recent realities of the real world. It seems rather the real world that neglects them.

Nor do I confess, thank heaven, to the more

odious vice of neglecting funny or frivolous fiction; whether in the sense of reading everything from the first story of Mr. Jacobs to the last story of Mr. Wodehouse; or in that richer sense in which the joke consists entirely of a corpse, a blood-stained hat-peg, or the mysterious footprints of a three-legged man in the garden. I have been a munificent patron of fiction of that description; and have even presented the public with a corpse or two of my own. In short, the limitation of my literary experience is altogether on the side of the modern serious novel; especially that very serious novel which is all about the psychology of flirting and jilting and going to jazz dances. I have read hundreds of books bearing titles like *Socialism: The Way Out*; or *Society: The Way In*; or *Japanese Light on the Paulus Mythus*; or *Cannibalism the Clue to Catholicism;* or *Parricide: A Contribution to Progress*; or *The Traffic Problem: The Example of Greenland*; or *Must We Drink?*; or *Should We Eat?*; or *Do We Breathe?* and all those grave and baffling questions. I have also read hundreds of books bearing titles like *Who Killed Humphrey Higgleswick?* or *The Blood on the Blotting-paper*; or *The Secret of Piccadilly Circus*; or *The Clue of the Stolen Toothbrush*; and so on and so on. But I have *not* read with sufficient regularity, diligence and piety all those other books that bear titles like

The Grasswidowhood of Grace Bellow; or *The Seventh Honeymoon of Sylphide Squeak*; or *Dear Lady Divorce*; or *The Sex of Samuel Stubbin*; or *Harold Hatrack, Soul-Thief*; or *The Hypnotist of Insomnia Smith*. All these grave and laborious, and often carefully written books come out season after season; and somehow I have missed them. Sometimes they miss me, even when hurled at my head by publishers. It were vain to deny that I sometimes deliberately avoid them. I have a reason, of a reasonable sort; for I do not think it is a really reasonable reason merely to say that they bore me. For I did once really try to read them; and I got lost. One reason is that I think there is in all literature a sort of purpose; quite different from the mere moralizing that is generally meant by a novel with a purpose. There is something in the plan of the idea that is straight like a backbone and pointing like an arrow. It is meant to go somewhere, or at least to point somewhere; to its end, not only in the modern sense of an ending, but in the medieval sense of a fruition. Now, I think that many of the less intellectual stories have kept this, where the more intellectual stories have lost it. The writer of detective stories, having once asked who killed Humphrey Higgleswick, must, after all, end by telling us who did it, even by the mean subterfuge of saying it was Humphrey Higgleswick. But the serious novelist asks a question that he does not answer; often that he is really incompetent to answer. The sex of Samuel Stubbin may even remain in considerable doubt, in some of the more emotional passages, and the seventh honeymoon of Sylphide seems to have nothing to do with the probable prospect of her eighth. It is the custom of these writers to scoff at the old sentimental novel or novelette, in which the story always ended happily to the sound of church bells. But, judged by the highest standards of heroic or great literature, like the Greek tragedies or the great epics, the novelette was really far superior to the novel. It set itself to reach a certain goal—the marriage of two persons, with all its really vital culmination in the founding of a family and a vow to God; and all other incidents were interesting because they pointed to a consummation which was, by legitimate hypothesis, a grand consummation.

But the modern refusal both of the religious vow and the romantic hope has broken the backbone of the business altogether, and it is only an assorted bag of bones. People are minutely described as experiencing one idiotic passion after another, passions which they themselves recognize as idiotic, and which even their own wretched philosophy forbids them to regard as steps towards any end. The sentimental novelette was a simplified and limited convention of the thing; in which, for the sake of argument, marriage was made the prize. Of course marriage is not the only thing that happens in life; and somebody else may study another section with another goal. But the modern serious novelists deny that there is any goal. They cannot point to the human happiness which the romantics associated with gaining the prize. They cannot point to the heavenly happiness which the religious associated with keeping the vow. They are driven back entirely on the microscopic description of these aimless appetites in themselves. And, microscopically studied in themselves, they are not very interesting to a middle-aged man with plenty of other things to think about. In short, the old literature, both great and trivial, was built on the idea that there is a purpose in life, even if it is not always completed in this life; and it really was interesting to follow the stages of such a purpose; from the meeting to the wedding, from the wedding to the bells, and from the bells to the church. But modern philosophy has taken the life out of modern fiction. It is simply dissolving into separate fragments and then into formlessness; and deserves much more than the romantic novel the modern reproach of being "sloppy."

XVII. ON LOGIC AND LUNACY

THE idea of logic is so entirely lost in this phase of philosophical history, that even those who invoke it do so rather as the Athenians once invoked the Unknown God, or the men of the Dark Ages retained a dim respect for Virgil as a conjurer. The very people who say, "be logical," will generally be found to be quite illogical in their own notion of logic. One of the last men who understood logic in its full and impartial sense, died only lately: the late William Johnson of King's College, Cambridge; one of the finest minds of the age and an exact measure of the modern contrast between notability and notoriety. I mean that somehow the glory has departed from glory, and the first men of the time are often the last men to be advertised or even adequately admired. He was as incapable of intellectual injustice as of infanticide; and while he and I differed about a thousand things, even if I had regarded his view as ultimately leading to falsehood, I should always have known that it was free from the faintest tinge of fallacy. If there had been any weed of weak logic in his own argument he would have torn it up with as much joy as any weed in the garden of the enemy.

For he liked that sort of weeding as an amusement and an art—a sort of art for art's sake. And when I wander in the jungle of journalistic nonsense in which we all live to-day, his memory again and again returns.

Let us begin with a trifle that does not matter in the least. He loved to argue about trifles that do not matter in the least. Some journalist the other day shook the foundation of the universe and the British Empire by raising the question of whether a girl ought to smoke a cigar. But what I noted about him, and about the hundred eager correspondents who pursued this great theme, was that they wrote again and again some such sentence as this: "If you like a girl to smoke a cigarette, why can't you be logical and like her to smoke a cigar?" Now I do not care an ounce of shag whether she smokes a cigarette or a cigar or a corn-cob pipe or a hubble-bubble, or whether she smokes three cigars at once, or whether she is an Anti-Tobacco crank. But it is none the less true that when a man writes that sentence telling us to "be logical," he shows that he has never even heard of the nature of logic. He might just as well write: "You like the look of a horse; why won't you be logical and like the look of a hippopotamus?" The only answer is, "Well, I don't"; and it is not illogical, because it does not in any way invade the realm of logic. A man has a perfect right to say that he likes the look of one thing and does not like the look of another thing; or even that he likes the look of a smaller thing, but does not like the look of a larger but somewhat similar thing. It is all a question of liking; and not in the least a question of logic. There is no logical compulsion upon him whatever to go on from the smaller to the larger and like them both. The man who uses this phrase attaches some queer particular meaning to the word "logical"; something that is dimly adumbrated in the words, "extremist" or "going the whole hog." But if my appetite is so small that I only require half a hog for breakfast, I am not any less of a logician because I refuse to eat the whole hog for breakfast. The obligation to eat the whole hog, if it exists, must be a mystical or moral or transcendental obligation; but it is not a logical obligation. It is not logical, because it has not been deduced from any premises; it has simply been stated without reference to any premises.

And that is what is the matter with the modern man who says, "be logical." He cannot take his own advice, and therefore he cannot state his own first principles. But though his logic is nonsense as he states it, it does refer to some first principles if he could only state them. It all depends on the *reason* for approving of cigarettes or cigars or girls or any other strange creatures. What he really means, at the back of his muddled modernistic mind, is something like this: "If I approve of Jennifer smoking a cigarette because Jennifer can jolly well do anything she likes, and does, *then* it is illogical in me to object to her liking a cigar; or for that matter an opium-pipe or a pint of laudanum or a bottle of prussic acid." And this statement would really be quite logical, because the logical reason is given. Or if he said, "It is my first principle that women may do anything that men do; *therefore* I am bound in logic to pass the cigars to my daughter as much as to my son," then that also is perfectly reasonable as the application of a stated principle. But to say that a man is bound in logic to like a cigar as much as a cigarette whether in his own mouth or that of his maiden aunt or his maternal grandmother, is stark staring unreason; and shows that the speaker is entirely illogical in dealing with the two ideas of liking and logic.

This half superstitious veneration for logic, combined with a complete misunderstanding of it, is very common in those popular works of fiction which are the joy of my existence; the crime novels and the police romances and the rest. There is a queer notion that the detective, who is distinguished from all human beings by having the gift of reason, is bound in logic not to like anything or anybody. Even Sherlock Holmes (the friend of my childhood to whom I shall always pay a tribute of piety) is described somewhere, I think, as being incapable of falling in love because of his logical nature. You might as well say that he could not be expected to have much appetite for lunch, because of his proficiency in mathematics. There is nothing intrinsically illogical in having affections or admirations or appetites, so long as we recognize them reasonably as what they are. But the romantic tradition, as it exists in all the romances, is that the logician cannot be romantic. It may be remarked that the word "cold" will always be found coupled with the word "logical"; I imagine the printers keep such words together in one block of type. But the cold logician, though he must not be romantic, is almost entirely a creature of romance. As a matter of fact and experience, most of the very logical people I have known have been very warm-blooded, affectionate or enthusiastic people. Most of the very good debaters were very warm debaters. Some of the closest reasoners in history were men of the most enthusiastic convictions; like St. Thomas Aquinas or the great French preachers and orators. The truth is, I think, that it was because the English were originally taught to have a prejudice against logic, that even when they half overcame the prejudice, there remained something alien in the admiration. They could be brought to feel a sort of awe in the presence of a really reasonable person; as if he were a sort of monster. The fact that a man could think could only be explained on the hypothesis that he was a Martian or the Man in the Moon; that he was a Clockwork Man; that he was The Thinking Machine. They began by thinking that reason is inhuman; and only gradually conceded that it is superhuman.

Is it not about time somebody preached the older doctrine; that reason is human? Is there not something to be said for those medieval Schoolmen and antiquated sages, who held that man is a rational animal; and even more rational than the other animals? The modern experiment of first sneering at logic for not being a practical thing, and then timidly praising it for being a priggish thing, seems to have resulted in the general loss of it as a normal function of the mind. It is as if the same Victorian English had supported their railway-trains by forbidding anybody to walk; and then, when all human limbs were paralysed, had deified two or three athletes as gods because they had the power of walking. Logic is as normal as legs; but legs can be neglected as well as logic. All that is needed is a little ordinary training and practice; the knowledge that inferences rest on their first principles, as men rest on their feet. But without it the world seems to be drifting into an intellectual dissolution and destruction, which is at its very wildest when some wild voice shrieks out of the chaos; "Be logical." This strange cry apparently means that you cannot stroke a cat without stroking a tiger; or that you are bound to wish the house was on fire because you sit by the fireside.

XVIII. ON THE THRILLS OF BOREDOM

It is a dogma imposed on all, by the dogmatic secularism of the modern system, that Youth needs, must have, and cannot possibly be happy without, a riot of dances, plays, or entertainments. We all know the practical truth embodied in this; and yet I am so doubtful about the fashionable assumption that I think it very nearly untrue. I have no objection to dances, plays, and masquerades: on the contrary, I enjoy them enormously; but then I am not what is commonly called a Youth. And from what I remember of being young, and what I have read of the real reminiscences of youth, I incline to think that youth never shows its glorious vividness and vitality so much as when transfiguring what might be called monotony. I feel far more sense of a creative glow, and of something passionately alive, in the description of the dreary moorland and dark mansion of the Brontës, or even of the dismal coffee-houses that were filled with the first dreams of Dickens, than I feel in the faces and conversation of half the young people I see at shows and dances today. Nor do I think it was a case of imagination existing in spite of dreariness; I think it existed in some degree because of dreariness. There is a psychological paradox here which perhaps only a poet can fully understand; but young people are generally poets.

I can recall in my childhood the continuous excitement of long days in which nothing happened; and an indescribable sense of fullness in large and empty rooms. And with whatever I retain of childishness (and whether it be a weakness or otherwise, I think I retain more than most) I still feel a very strong and positive pleasure in being stranded in queer quiet places, in neglected corners where nothing happens and anything may happen; in unfashionable hotels, in empty waiting-rooms, or in watering-places out of the season. It seems as if we needed such places, and sufficient solitude in them, to let certain nameless suggestions soak into us and make a richer soil of the subconsciousness. Certainly, if there is such a need, it is a need that is now being everywhere neglected. Of course, all such views of youth or childhood or the past are a matter of proportion. Children did not like thrashings or even threatenings; they did not all like thunderstorms; they did not like solitude or darkness or horrors increased beyond their capacity for supporting them. But, allowing for that, the normal little boy likes solitude and loves horrors. Only, as I say, there is a fine shade that goes even beyond this, and suggests something of sustenance even in which many would now call merely stuffy and stagnant. The imagination can not only enjoy darkness; it can even enjoy dullness. I know that men like Dickens, writing recollections, have complained of dullness. But when I read their recollections, I doubt if they were ever for one instant dull. It must have been in those very hours that there first began that dance of the Dickens characters after which the world need never be dull again.

In that dance of Dickens characters, I trust I need not explain that I do not figure either as Mr. Stiggins the Puritan or Mr. Scrooge the Utilitarian. I have not the smallest intention of interfering with anybody's dances or dramatic entertainments; and, in due proportion, I am prepared to interfere with any interference. But there is a moral and mental fact involved, which is being neglected in the concentration on communal or convivial enjoyment; and that fact consists precisely in the real vitality and power of youth. Youth is much more capable of amusing itself than is now supposed, and in much less mortal need of being amused. The only real warning against solitude and stagnation which needs to be uttered is that you do really need to be rather young and strong in order to get the fun out of them. The same principle applies to the monastic life; a career that requires very great vigour and vivacity. No normal person is expected to be so vigorous and vivacious as that. But most normal persons are now taught to neglect far too much the sort of excitement which the mind itself manufactures out of unexciting things. And anybody who can feel the fine shades, in fiction or philosophy will agree that the old school called Romantic, or even Byronic, which we feel still volcanic in the Brontës, had really about it a curious confidence in life, an unbroken hope in the heart, which is strangely stubborn in many people who had been as badly brought up as Byron. Byron himself, with all his parade of pessimism, had a sort of glamour of life about him that he could not get rid of, and a gusto that never left his language, even when he used it to deny its existence in his life.

Now, one need not belong to the extreme school of The Nightmare of the Night Club, or Vengeance on the Vamp, in order to observe around us a certain lack of that really romantic gusto and glamour. To mention another Dickens character, it will be remembered that the Infant Phenomenon was kept short by means of gin, so that she might go on dancing as a light and airy child. It seems to me that a good many people are kept from growing by cocktails, and stunted rather than stimulated by dancing. They are not allowed to grow, because they are always pulling themselves up by the roots to see how they are growing. In the case of those who really have a heat and force of generous youth within them, I seriously think that imprisonment in a second-rate boarding-house during a rainy day at Worthing, or enforced retirement to a faded and forgotten tea-shop off the road to Wormwood Scrubs, would lead to their returning to their friends younger than ever. As to those who are already dried up, hopeless, cynical, and filled with intellectual despair, they can continue to be gay.

This need is a normal need; like other normal needs, it can be neglected for a period; like other normal needs, it will certainly be rediscovered at a later period. Perhaps it will be discovered incidentally and individually; perhaps it will be discovered darkly and secretly, as by the conspirators of individualism or the revolutionists of tradition. Perhaps the plotters will whisper to each other, amid the whirl of the latest jazz or ragtime, the forbidden assignation and the address of the Worthing boarding-house. Perhaps a solitary figure will be seen slinking from the Scarlet Cuttlefish (that exclusive night club) and grimly taking the road to Wormwood Scrubs. Perhaps, on the other hand, it will come with a communal rush like the return of a fashion; and it will be all the rage to be found sitting speechless in a waiting-room at Willesden Junction; and all the best people will leave themselves lying about, like so much lost luggage, in the parlours of dilapidated public-houses or on the steps of derelict bathing-machines at dead Victorian resorts. These are the only places I can think of in which a modern man and women could possibly have time or opportunity to think for themselves. These are the modern equivalents of sitting among the ruins or meditating among the tombs; and both were very healthy human exercises, very improving to the spirits.

In this connexion, by the way, I must once more express my astonishment that, in an age which will have ten professors of psychology to tea, or strew the world with pamphlets and books about subconsciousness and psycho-analysis, nobody seems to notice the most normal and elementary facts of practical psychology. Otherwise, it would not be left to an irresponsible and ignorant journalist to point out the elementary fact: that dullness can be a stimulant. There is hardly any need to point out, to any one acquainted with our lighter entertainments, that amusement can be a narcotic. But, anyhow, some one with more scientific authority ought really to study these strange reactions of stale and even oppressive atmospheres on the romantic spirit of youth. Who knows?—if something suggestive were written on the subject, even youth might be young once more.

XIX. ON GOSSIP ABOUT HEREDITY

A SHORT time ago a distinguished scientific expert, pleading for a more normal and less panic-stricken treatment of consumptives, summed up one aspect in the decisive words: "Consumption is no more hereditary than measles." He said, of course, that it could attack successive members of the same family, and for the same reasons as measles. I have no authority to speak on the technical point; but a statement like this, which may fairly be called authoritative, turns my mind back on the vast and sprawling treatment of the topic of heredity, in popular science and public opinion. And, though I do not claim to know much about the medical facts or falsehoods set forth in this particular case, I rather think I do know something of the moral facts and falsehoods that lie behind them and are their sole and continuous motive-power. There are undoubtedly individual professors, who fight each other on tiny points out of pure impersonal curiosity, or possibly out of pure personal dislike. But when any part of the general public is drawn into a debate on physical science, we may be certain that it has already become a debate on moral science. Mobs are always moral.

There never was a mob that rose to demand the squaring of the circle or the closer observation of the Transit of Venus. Professor Higgle and Professor Haggle may argue the hind-leg off a donkey, or the hundredth leg off a centipede, to settle a question that nobody can understand but themselves. But if ever the dancing donkey and the writhing centipede become heraldic figures on the flags and ensigns of the crowd, then we may be quite certain that for some sort of reason (probably quite an unreasonable reason) these biological questions have somehow been entangled with faith and morals; and that what is raging in the street is the war of two philosophies.

Now, almost as soon as the word "heredity" was invented or spoken aloud, it was caught up like a cry in the market-place, and repeated in every variation of gossip and chattering comment; applied to this, that, and the other, to which it was never in any case applicable; and trumpeted aloud by men who did not even know what it meant, long before even the most learned men knew even the little about it that they know now. Mendel the monk has explained it much more fully than did Darwin and all the material scientists; but even after that it remains a very obscure and subtle subject, as the scientists would be the first to admit.

But in the great days when Science was also

Fashion, when the world had to bow down not only to Darwin, but to all Darwinians, when anything labelled "Specimens" or "Sections" passed without challenge, and all the camp-followers of materialism were sacred, like the suite of an Embassy—in those days of one idea or one tendency there arose the most amazing fashion of talking about Heredity. It was simply taken for granted, for instance, in a hundred provincial homes that what they called Drink was hereditary. If they had used language in a rational manner they might have been quite right, for the disposition to drink something is a hereditary human instinct; and the objection to doing so, when it happens to be beer, is a superficial, artificial, and self-conscious pose. But what they meant was alcoholism; and what they meant was nonsense. Nobody has ever tasted alcohol. Nobody in the normal way has ever seen it. Nobody most certainly has ever liked it. What people liked was a certain pleasure, either of excitement or serenity, which can be gained through a variety of liquids, moderately by moderate indulgence, or excessively by excessive indulgence. Alcohol is simply a name which professors give (for the present) to some elements in all these liquids which they suppose (for the present) to be the cause of this mental pleasure. Now, it is obvious on the face of it that, if anything is hereditary, it cannot be a craving for the chemical process, which most people do not even know to exist. It can only be a craving for the mental result, which is simple pleasure. Now, all men have a craving for pleasure; and, though some men are weaker or more wilful in snatching at it, I cannot for the life of me see why such men should not snatch at other pleasures as much as this one. If what is inherited is anything so vague as a lack of vigilance and self-control against pleasure itself, I cannot see why the drunkard should not have one son who was a jewel-thief and another who was always flirting with barmaids or bolting with ballet-girls. Of course, many children of drunken families are drunken; not because there is heredity, but because there are a great many other things besides heredity. There is such a thing as tradition, which is nearly half of true history; and there is such a thing as suggestion, which is nearly all of modern journalism; and there are such things as education and environment, about which a still louder yell of human folly will go up—in short, there is something in morals which corresponds to infection in measles.

But this wild romance of popular science spread wider and wider. What is odd about it is not its truth or untruth, but the unresisted smoothness with which it spread over one field after another. I know so little of the scientific study itself that I should not think of denying the possibility of some sort of inherited drunkenness; though I cannot make any sense of the theory of inherited alcoholism. But why were hundreds and thousands of people, who knew even less science than I do, instantly and calmly assured that drunkenness was hereditary? Why did they begin at once at watch the doubtful steps of the curate, because his great-uncle the Admiral was found drunk in a ditch on Trafalgar Day? Why did they eagerly watch for the fire of alcoholic craving in the eyes of the new-born infant who was remotely descended from Three-Bottle Thumpington? The question grows wilder as the application grew wider. The next thing we heard was the cheerful news that Assassination was a regular family feature, like a family nose. As in the other cases, it was not so much stated by scientific people as spread by unscientific people as the last scientific news. A brilliant lady novelist lately based a whole novel upon it, called *Red Sky at Morning,* in which a hazy, good-natured youth kills somebody for a very insufficient reason, merely because his father fifty years ago had killed somebody quite different for a totally different reason. All this seems to me highly irrational. There are almost as many motives for murdering men as there are men to murder. A man kills because he is blackmailed, or because he is jilted, or because he is a political fanatic, and so on. But how do you inherit a blackmailer, or an unreliable girl, or a political theory? There certainly is inheritance, as of physical type, perhaps of physical temperament; of being indolent or restless and so on. But the number of lazy men who will murder a valet for waking them up is about as large as the number of impatient men who will murder him for keeping them waiting. That is to say, it is very small. The mysterious moral inhibition, or its absence, by which men do or do not murder, is in the individual soul; and I defy anybody to show that it is hereditary.

What is the meaning of this popular superstition? In existing relations of religion and good taste, I can only suggest it in a parable. On the highest and hoariest of the ashpits of hell sits the oldest of all the Demons, whose name is Doom; it is he who has always blighted mankind with superstitions of the destiny and death of races; who told the old Greeks like Œdipus that they were bound to their blind crimes; who told the old feudal tribes that there was a curse on a castle or an abortion that was the burden of a family. And when modern science said "Heredity" the old fiend stirred, and saw a new chance of renewing the old bondage. For however we take the symbols, it was a wise instinct by which heaven was symbolized by wings that are free as the wind, and hell symbolized by chains.

XX. ON DANTE AND BEATRICE

THE interesting, one might almost say amusing, idea of "The Poets on the Poets," the series published by Messrs. Faber and Faber, is described by those playful publishers themselves as based "on the impudent maxims, 'Set a Poet to catch a Poet' and 'Bards of a feather flock together.' " I am not sure that the latter motto is so exact as the former. Thus Mr. Humbert Wolfe is to write on Tennyson; and it would never have occurred to me that those two excellent bards had a single feather between them. But the former maxim is sound enough, and is well supported by the second of the series, in which an illuminating sketch of Dante is presented by Mr. T. S. Eliot.

In such cases we are all of us only picking up stray feathers here and there, as Browning picked up the eagle's feather on the heath. Mr. T. S. Eliot would be the last to pretend that he had completely plucked the eagle of Florence and Ravenna. If it is not easy to write a short book about Dante, neither is it easy to write a short article about Mr. Eliot. As he naturally picks out two or three of Dante's ideas, I can only pick out one or two of his own ideas, and the subject-matter necessarily narrows from the poet to the critic and from the critic to the critic of the critic. But all his ideas are both stimulating and subtle, including any number I have no space to estimate here. Perhaps the most outstanding matter, in a popular sense, is his very just reconstruction of the business about the story of Beatrice, as she appears not only in the *Divine Comedy*, but in the *Vita Nuova*. There has always been a controversy about Beatrice, and as so often happens (I grieve to say) in the controversies of the very learned, a mass of the most extraordinary nonsense has been talked on both sides. At one extreme there was the school of those who pretended that Beatrice was in the position of Mrs. Harris; or that she was, at best (to quote another great female authority), an allegory on the banks of the Nile: at any rate, hardly human enough to have ever been on the banks of the Arno. Some of them said she was a symbol standing for Theology or Divine Wisdom or some such thing; others, from colleges even nearer Hanwell, said she was an allegory of United Italy or Liberty or the League of Nations or heaven knows what. About that, especially in the case of the *Vita Nuova* (though I am not learned, and hardly even educated, touching Italian language and letters), I have not myself the shadow of a doubt. The man—

or, rather, boy—who remembered with such scorching delight the fact that a little girl had nodded and smiled at him on a particular morning, and with such scorching despair the fact that she had not nodded or smiled at him on another morning, was most certainly in love. It was first love, calf-love, moon-calf-love, no doubt, but certainly human love; and if it wasn't I will modestly exclaim with Shakespeare, "I never writ nor no man ever loved." And that Dante does mean the same young woman to reappear in the *Paradiso* is obvious, not only from many phrases in the *Paradiso,* but from the quite definite words at the end of the *Vita Nuova.* But when the opposite extreme of criticism suggests that human love is the whole subject of both books, then, as Mr. Eliot shows, it makes even worse nonsense out of the whole business.

For the Romantics of the ninteenth century really implied that God and the Universe, Heaven, Hell, and Purgatory, were all one elaborate and rather laborious compliment to Beatrice Portinari. It is truer to say that, in the true sense, Beatrice is a compliment to God. She is lifted like flowers on an altar, or flames on a candlestick, to be an example of that earthly beauty which, used rightly, can lead us to heavenly beauty. And in this case the critics have missed the whole point of the comparison between the *Vita Nuova* and the *Divine Comedy.* The point is that the first slight, youthful, merely emotional story is really a sad story; it is only the completion in Paradise that is a joyful story. The former has an unhappy ending—or, rather, that most unhappy ending which consists in having no ending. It is the mere fragment of a human tragedy; it is only the religious epic that is, in the exact sense, a divine comedy. Dante is drawn as a dark and bitter spirit; but in fact he wrote the only one of the great epics that really has a happy ending.

The trouble was that the age of the Romantics was the age of the Rationalists, or those who thought they were Rationalists. Having figured as ruthless realists sweeping all spiritual visions like cobwebs out of the sky, they then suddenly became extravagant sentimentalists over some of the common or garden flowers they found growing naturally out of the earth. Having forbidden all belief in the legend of Adam and Eve, they demanded universal and absolute belief in the legend of Edwin and Angelina. They were not content with the natural sympathy we all have with such natural feelings; they really gave to them the supremacy of supernatural feelings—and (what is the real point) the *only* supernatural feelings. They did not use the coarse cant of our day; but they did, in fact, make Sex the supreme end of life for its own sake—in which they were much less sensible than the common or garden flowers. They therefore missed the whole meaning of Dante, which is that human love may indeed be a new life; but the new life must be dedicated to a supreme good as much as the old life. All other goods are only manifestations of that supreme good, and must ultimately be referred to it, as Beatrice to the Beatific Vision.

There is one comment, in this connexion, which occurred to me while reading Mr. Eliot's book. The Beatific Vision is described by Dante about as well as it could be described by anybody—that is, chiefly by saying that it cannot be described at all. But Mr. Eliot has noticed, as I have often noticed, the very extraordinary effect of the ending, when, after a few grand hints (like that about a happy but forgotten dream), the poet suddenly introduces the vast but seemingly very distant simile about how Neptune must have felt when the Argo first sailed over him. At first sight it seems quite out of the picture; and yet for the imaginative it is right on the spot. Now there seem to be a number of these abrupt and abysmal irrelevancies in Dante's poetry, and, indeed, in all great poetry. They seem to be suggesting a vivid image by suddenly introducing a totally different image. Instead of saying that Beatrice looked beautiful, Dante says that he felt like Glaucus when he ate the grass that made him sea-fellow of the gods. I do not know why that dim heathen dream delights me, but it does; much more, probably, than the best direct description of Beatrice's beauty. It seems as if the sudden presentation of some quite remote vision, as imaginative as the main image, completes it and makes it convincing. There are many examples in other poets, including the rather hackneyed example of Keats, when he broke off a reasonably intelligent discourse on the nightingale to talk about perilous seas and magic casements, with which nightingales have nothing whatever to do. Like Dante, he had got beyond himself, and irrelevancy was the only expression of imagination. But there is something else in it relevant to Mr. Eliot's thesis. This summoning of remote symbols, this calling of spirits from the vasty deep, like the sea-green Glaucus into the presence of Beatrice, does suggest something involved in the theology of the matter. It suggests that *all* beautiful images are shadows of the one real beauty, and can be, in a sense, shifted or interchanged for its service. It prevents *mere* fixed idolatry of one shadow in one mirror, as if it were the origin of all. Beatrice is to be loved because she is beautiful; but she is beautiful because there is behind her a many-sided mystery of beauty, to be seen also in the grass and the sea, and even in the dead gods. There is a promise in and yet beyond all such pictures; and the poet can see grass or the great sea or the great ship going over it, hearing a sort of whisper: "Thine eyes shall see the King in his beauty."

XXI. ON QUACKS IN THE HOME

CAN anything be done to dam, not to say damn, the deluge of Quackery that is now being poured out everywhere to inform what is called the ignorance of the democracy? As the term implies, it is not only democracy that is ignorant. Those who would inform it are more ignorant still, or they would not invariably say the democracy when they mean the demos. Democracy does not mean the populace, or even the people; it means government by the people. Democracy is a very noble thing, and it does not exist—at any rate at present. Demos is a very jolly thing in its way, especially when it does all the things that ideal democrats generally abuse it for doing, such as drinking, shouting, and going to the Derby. But, whatever else it is doing, it is not ruling: it is not teaching, but being taught. And there might be a reasonable case for its being taught, were it not for the unfortunate fact that it is being taught tosh. Which brings me back, after this parenthesis on the word democracy, to the more solemn and sacred subject of Quackery.

Quackery is false science; it is everywhere apparent in cheap and popular science; and the chief mark of it is that men who begin by boasting that they have cast away all dogmas go on to be incessantly, impudently, and quite irrationally dogmatic. Let any one run his eye over any average newspaper or popular magazine, and note the number of positive assertions made in the name of popular science, without the least pretence of scientific proof, or even of any adequate scientific authority. It is all the worse because the dogmas are generally concerned with domestic and very delicate human relations; with heredity and home environment; and everything that can be coloured by the pompous and pretentious polysyllables of Psychology and Education. At least many of the old dogmas, right or wrong, were concerned with cherubim and seraphim, with lost spirits and beatified souls; but these dogmas always directly attack fathers and wives and children, without offering either credentials or evidence. The general rule is that nothing must be accepted on any ancient or admitted authority, but everything must be accepted on any new or nameless authority, or accepted even more eagerly on no authority at all. It is quite satisfactory, of course, if any nobody says in any newspaper: "Dr. Binns, of Buffalo, has told us that, while aunts may be fond of nephews, great-aunts always have an instinctive hatred and aversion both for nephews and nieces." But it is even more convincing than that if the information is anonymous in every way, and the writer merely states: "Recent science has shown that second cousins are naturally antagonistic, but that in second cousins once removed, the antagonism is sometimes introverted into suicidal mania." Where all these statements come from nobody knows. Where they all go to everybody ought to know, since they go to everybody. But it is in practice very difficult to discover what becomes of them, and whether they are really treated as wisdom or waste paper. On the whole, I fear it is more likely that everybody believes them than that anybody takes the trouble to check them.

This evil is wilder in America, but I doubt if it is worse in America. It is scattered all over our own Press and public speech, and is all the more insidious because it is not so much associated with the conspicuous figures of picturesque charlatans and fantastic prophets, such as strut in strange plumage about the plains of the West. Anyhow, it is scattered so widely both here and there that the difficulty is to pick up any adequate example. For the triviality of one specimen does not convey the tremendous and mountainous multitude of specimens. Here is one example, however, which I find in a periodical of considerable intellectual pretensions, to judge by its title. Like most of these professed organs of thought, it is marked by a complete incapacity for any precision in thinking. But I mention it, not because it is worse than the rest, but because it is representative of the rest and all the rest are no better. The instructor informs us that there can be between parent and child a *negative transference* (the intense italics are his), which seems to mean, not merely that the child will hate the parent, but that the child will love somebody who is the opposite of the hated parent. "Thus a child who is treated coldly by his mother will come to reject all people like his mother and seek for her opposite. We will say the mother is good, honest, moral, even pious. The boy will gravitate to some one crooked, immoral, or even wicked. In short, his mother's goodness may send him to the devil, though all the time she may be wondering why her excellent precepts, her discipline, her goodness are failing to develop like traits in her son."

You will note the utter chaos of terminology and definition, even in these few lines. Some of us, to begin with, might hesitate to insist on the goodness of a mother who treated a child coldly. But what is meant by the mother being good, as distinct from her being moral? What is meant by the mother's mysterious rival being immoral, as distinct from being wicked? And what in the name of goodness (or morality) is meant by the mysterious word "even," which is reserved only for wickedness and for piety? The transference of these thoughts, from writer to reader, is a very negative transference indeed. However, the writer, having said that the mother's goodness, which seems to be the same as her coldness, may send the boy to the devil, goes on to say that it may be a good thing that he should go to the devil; in which case it was presumably a good thing that the mother should be cold. Revolt, we are told, sometimes leads to new ways of life, and it may be highly satisfactory that the boy should seek for the opposite of his mother. But what *is* the opposite of your mother? As a point of logic, it seems rather subtle; nor does the logician here instructing us give us very much help. "A rebel boy may, of course, become, like the proverbial minister's son, a good-for-naught or a crook; on the other hand, a boy like Balzac, who hated his practical father, became a great novelist—his father's opposite. Or in a different way, Beethoven, whose father was a poor fiddler, a drunkard and ne'er-do-well, became one of the great composers of the world, doggedly determined to protect his mother and be as unlike his father as possible." If that was his object, we can hardly say that he succeeded very well. I am not quite sure what is the opposite of a poor fiddler, but certainly it is not a great composer. There may be many a great composer who has been a poor fiddler, and many a poor fiddler who may yet be a great composer. The same mysterious use of the word "opposite" darkens the other instance given from the career of Balzac. I cannot understand why, in logic, a great novelist is the exact contrary of a practical father. I do not see why any child may not happen to rejoice in the possession of a great practical novelist-father. The children of Sir Walter Scott, for instance, to a great extent did so, despite the accident which ruined his later fortunes. But it is not only false in the typical case of Scott, it is far from true even in the actual case of Balzac. Balzac had a decidedly "practical" side to him; he was not only busy, but business-like, in his own way; and, anyhow, all these crude contrasts about complex characters are all nonsense. Balzac did not become a great novelist because his father had annoyed him with practicality; he became a great novelist because he was a great man. Beethoven did not succeed because his father drank; it is much more likely that he was a composer for the same reason that made his father a fiddler. These are only a few random examples of these random statements which are thrown about everywhere, that the people may learn Science from men who have never learnt Logic. Now that everybody is talking about the public being informed of this or that, is there any way of stopping the public being misinformed in this endless and exuberant fashion?

XXII. ON A GENERALLY ACCEPTED MISTAKE

THE current cant, which is a cant against cant, has produced a crop of modern proverbs, or phrases, which everybody repeats for the hundredth time and nobody examines for the first time, or they would instantly be found to be false. A typical case is that which we have all heard again and again in some such form as this: "In every age people have thought their own time prosaic and only the past poetical. If you think the medieval or any other period picturesque, that is only the glamour of antiquity; men in those days felt about them as you do about these days. Their costumes and customs were as dull and trivial to them as yours are to you." The maxim appeals in many ways to the modern mind; it merges something with something else; it levels downwards; it contradicts the claims of chivalry and religious devotion; it is comforting and it is entirely untrue.

Mr. Rudyard Kipling, always the poet of this popular modernity, has summarized the notion admirably in a poem about Romance being at all times actually in the present and apparently in the past—a poem beginning, I think:

> "Farewell, Romance," the cavemen cried,
> With bone and flint he went away.

I need hardly say that there is not a grain of anything remotely resembling evidence that the cavemen ever cried anything of the sort. It is one of the thousand things which are said about them because there is no evidence either way. But there are tons of evidence that the earliest men whose motives we can follow regarded their own rituals and traditions as reasonably dignified. There have been periods in which poets and satirists have said that society was degenerating through luxury or laxity, and many periods in which they were perfectly right in saying so. There have been some periods—not very many—in which men have been intensely interested in some special period of the past. So the men of the Renaissance vaguely regarded antiquity as a heroic age. But they did not regard their own as a prosaic age. Shakespeare might be thrilled by Plutarch's tales of great men in togas and tunics; but that did not prevent him from conceiving Hamlet as an ordinary Elizabethan gentleman, fencing with rapier and dagger, wearing probably a ruff and almost certainly a beard. Every modern man, when he first heard of Hamlet in modern dress, felt a faint shiver of doubt; even if he was sympathetic, he feared that it might be comic. But Shakespeare probably did conceive Hamlet in modern dress—in his modern dress. And there is nothing to show that he thought it in the least comic.

The truth is that *no* other age except the nineteenth century (and perhaps our little bit of the twentieth) ever did regard its own dress and habits as ugly and undignified. The thing can be tested in a hundred ways, and one is even tolerably familiar. Sensational French artists, in the nineteenth century, deliberately and defiantly painted pictures from the Gospel in modern dress, with Christ standing among men in trousers and top-hats. It was purposely done to "shock" the Salon; needless to say, it would have been far too shocking for the Royal Academy. Yet it was not the first time the thing had been done. It was only the first time it had been thought shocking. There is not a single one of the previous epochs of Christian art, from the stiffest primitive Byzantine to the last realism of the Venetians or Dutch, when artists had not painted the Gospel scenes with the dress and habits of their own time. It is not, in plain fact, a question of why men think the present fashion ugly and the past fashion beautiful. It is a question of why they think this of trousers and top-hats, when they did *not* think it of trunk-hose or togas or tunics. Many subtle explanations might be suggested; but I incline myself to suspect that the dark secret can, after all, be stated more simply. Might I tentatively suggest that top-hats and trousers give us this uncanny impression of ugliness because they are ugly? Might I suggest that the mercantile nineteenth century thought itself hideous because it was hideous?—and the perception did credit to its acumen and even to its humility.

In short, there was a moment in the middle of the nineteenth century which was the midnight of artistic instinct, just as there was a moment about the middle of the ninth century which was the midnight of law and organization. It was blackest in a commercial country like England, which was only saved by treating itself as comic because it could not treat itself as dignified. It produced, for instance, the figure of the policeman, who was so comic that he had to be put at once into a pantomime, because he could not be put into a pageant. But almost any other age or country would have clad and armed the city guard so as to be an ornament to any pageant. Our age was ugly and undignified; our nation was redeemed by the national sense of humour that at least would not pretend to be dignified. The things of that period are all stamped with the insignia of indignity. It is not true that this is affected by it being a past or a present period. Mr. Kipling himself in the poem quoted, gave the case away by saying that "Romance brought up the nine-fifteen," implying that the clerks in the train did not yet realize their own romance. But since that was written steam has grown old compared to petrol, as stage-coaches grew old compared to steam. Yet taking a third-class ticket at Euston Station is not much more wildly poetic now than it was when railways ruled the land. Steam may grow stale, but it does not grow specially poetical. If the old coach was faintly poetical, it was because a faint tradition of quite another sort lingered with the ancient echoes of the horse and of the horn. If the railway carriage does not turn into a romantic ruin before our eyes, it is because there lingers in it a nameless something of the nineteenth century: something that was proud of being prosaic and rigidly refuses to be anything else. It is the stamp of that particularly barbarous interlude: the *only* age in history when men dared not put the Twelve Apostles in modern dress.

This particular matter, in which the medieval world differed from the modern, must be clearly understood to start with, for instance, as one of the conditions governing *The Canterbury Tales*. The creative imagination of Chaucer could do much; it could do much more than it is commonly credited with doing; but it could hardly have bridged the abyss between the sublime and the ridiculous which yawned in the imagination of a man of the nineteenth century. Chaucer did not regard his own age as comic and commonplace. He regarded some people in it as comic, and some, perhaps, as commonplace; but the clothes and externals of these people could be used just as easily to express what was most imaginative and ideal. The Knight as described, might have figured in any medieval picture as kneeling all clad in iron on one side of an enthroned Virgin and Child; his crusading spirit belongs altogether to that more remote region of delicate distances and golden clouds. But he is not out of the picture of *The Canterbury Tales,* nor of any medieval picture in which there might be grotesque dwarfs or gambolling dogs. But he would be out of the picture called "The Derby Day," by Frith. That picture contains considerable variety; but it does not contain the Knight of *The Canterbury Tales.* For "The Derby Day" was painted at that midnight moment of art when even the artist did not think that the world he saw was artistic. This unnatural sense of ugliness is so much our immediate inheritance that there are ordinary words that have never recovered from it. The very word "hat" has a hazy air of farce about it; mentioned by itself it suggests first the hat of Charlie Chaplin or the admirable song of "Where Did You Get That Hat?" The first lesson in medievalism is to understand that Chaucer did not feel about the word "hood" as we do about the word "hat." He knew there were knavish people who carried two faces under one hood; but the one face might be that of Friar Francis as well as of Friar Tuck. A halo round a hood did not seem queer, like a halo round a hat, for those who think only of modern hats. There had been plenty of preposterous fashions among the rich in Chaucer's time, but their very limitations to the rich had left the landscape and colour-scheme of medievalism more or less what it is in the simplest medieval pictures. There was preposterous costume in that age, but he did not think all costume preposterous because it was of that age. He was as ready to be humorous in verse as any serious poet who ever lived, but his head was not filled with an endless, derisive echo of "Where Did You Get that Hood?"

XXIII. ON THE LATER PORTIONS OF POEMS

SOMETIMES I have a dark suspicion that there are many poems, and perhaps prose competitions also, which people think they know when they know only the first few lines. Possibly this might explain the sinister haste and eagerness with which the great Epic Poets cram into the first few lines a statement of the whole story, which they intend to tell in the ensuing twelve books. They always begin with a summary of this kind, perhaps because they have a craven fear that many of their readers will not read any more. Everybody knows the first three lines of *Paradise Lost:*

> Of man's first disobedience and the fruit
> Of that forbidden Tree, whose mortal taste
> Brought death into the world and all our woe.

But I strongly suspect that there is a sudden and enormous falling off in the numbers of those who could quote the fourth line. And Milton may himself have paused at that point, and heaved a sigh of relief, to think that he had got the whole story packed pretty thoroughly into the three lines, even if all his readers refused to read him any more. He had successfully informed the public of the incident called "The Fall of Man," had explained its connexion with the fruit of the Tree of Knowledge, and attached to it all the results of the doctrine of Original Sin. He did not, however, stop here, and leave this little trifle as a sort of epigram or short lyric. He went on for quite a long time; and it must have been with a sense of relief, not unmingled with fatigue, that he reached at last that quiet and beautiful ending, and saw the exiles, hand in hand, with faltering steps and slow, through Eden take their solitary way. It is perhaps an advantage to the epic poets that their story, as a rule, is already more or less known to the public; just as a considerable number of people have heard the story of Adam and Eve. All adventure stories, in Stevenson's phrase, begin to end well; and in the greatest of adventure stories Ulysses is obviously meant to get home at last; nor are there many people who need to read to the end of the *Iliad* to find out what happened to Hector. In the case of longer and more elaborate, not to say more entangled, poems, like those of Ariosto and Spenser, it is legitimate to doubt whether everybody does know what happened to anybody. Lord Macaulay was the most persistent of readers, with the most perfect of memories; yet it is admitted that he came a cropper, or fell out of the race, in the forests of the *Faërie Queene*. He said that few readers were in at the death of the Blatant Beast, and if he had been there himself he would have known that the Beast does not even die. But while this lack of final perseverance is common in the case of the complicated epics, and not uncommon in that of the simpler epics, it may seem almost cynical to suggest that it is sometimes true even of shorter poems. It seems heartless to suggest that somebody may have fainted before he got to the end of "We Are Seven." It is awful to think that some critic may have been so fastidious as to be unable to support more than two lines of "The Village Blacksmith." And yet I fancy there are cases in which something like this is true; and I came across one recently, or rather I only recently fancied that I saw the true meaning of it.

Everybody quotes the opening lines of Shelley's fine chorus of "Hellas." And everybody quotes them as the expression of Shelley's heroic hope for the human race, his idealism and his optimism about his ideals, his radiant faith in a final fulfilment in which humanity should be happy and free:

> The world's great age begins anew,
> The golden years return.

And I suspect that of these a very considerable number have not read, or do not remember, or did not understand, the curious breaking-point which is the point of the poem. I have read it hundreds of times myself, but I confess that it was not until lately that I saw its full meaning, in connexion with cosmic and philosophical theories. I dare say everybody else who has read it understood it much better and more immediately; I am not setting up as a discoverer, but I do think it curious that the discovery has not been more often rediscovered. Shelley's poem mounts steadily in an ascending curve of choral thanksgiving to Nature for a new and glorious renovation of all things; and then, when it comes to its highest note of triumph, it breaks. The poet cries, with something like horror, that we must look no further and foresee no more:

> O, drain not to the dregs the urn
> Of bitter prophecy.

It is obvious, to put it mildly, that something has occurred to him to put him out. And though all readers must have realized at least that, I fancy there have been a considerable number of quoters who were not readers. And I do not think that Shelley's name would have been so innocently and irrevocably bound up with ideas of Progress and Perfectibility and A Good Time Coming, if everybody had instantly realized to what he really referred.

This very obvious reflection, which must have occurred to hundreds of people, occurred to me when I was in the act of reading that very remarkable historical study called *Progress and Religion,* by Christopher Dawson, which Messrs. Sheed & Ward published some little time ago. It contains, among many other interesting things, a very complete account of that extraordinary theory of Recurrence, which many modern as well as ancient philosophers have held, but to which the ancient philosophers gave the name of "The Great Year." The theory, of course, is broadly this: that when all possible permutations and combinations have been exhausted, the cosmic system will of its nature have to begin all over again and repeat everything we know exactly as we have known it. This will happen again and again for ever; for the same logic that brings the repetition must also bring the repetition of the repetition. And, indeed, it is odd to notice how the philosophers repeat themselves even in describing the repetition. Mr. Dawson quotes the case of a Greek sage who said, "This staff that I am holding I shall hold again," and the case of a Socialist thinker who said, "This pen I am holding I shall hold again," in almost exactly the same form of words. Every detail of every life will return with exactitude, and return again and again to eternity. And everybody knows how Nietzsche uttered this revelation, with something almost like a howl, from the last high and crazy peak of his strange existence; about the time, indeed, when he collapsed into complete insanity. I do not know whether he went mad because he believed the theory, or only believed the theory because he went mad. But it always struck me as an almost startling example of how a deathly fatalism overcomes the most lively sceptic. For Nietzsche's views, in his best days, were wild enough, but wild at least on the side of Will and of Liberty. To see him entangled in that old necessitarian net is like seeing a great spider's web entangle an eagle.

What interests me here is that it entangled the skylark as well as the eagle. It is surely obvious that Shelley, in the rise and fall of those remarkable lines of the Hellas Chorus, is referring to the old pagan conception of The Great Year. He feels that it justifies him in saying that the world's great age will begin anew and the golden years return. But he does not want to drain the urn of prophecy to the dregs, because the same wheel of fate that has brought round the golden years will bring round also the leaden and the iron years; and we shall all be forced to repeat all the crimes and tyrannies of history. Without being unduly controversial, I think I may say that it is not a cheery prospect. And I am exceedingly proud to observe that it was before the coming of Christianity that it flourished, and after the neglect of Christianity that it returned.

XXIV. ON THE ROMANCE OF CHILDHOOD

I AM just old enough to remember the world before telephones. And I remember that my father and my uncle fitted up with their own metal and chemicals the first telephone I ever saw: a miniature telephone reaching from the top bedroom under the roof to the remote end of the garden. I was really impressed imaginatively by this; and I do not think I have ever been so much impressed since by any extension of it. The point is rather important in the whole theory of imagination. It did startle me that a voice should sound in the room when it was really as distant as the next street. It would hardly have startled me more if it had been as distant as the next town. It does not startle me any more if it is as distant as the next continent. The miracle is over. Thus I admired even the large scientific things most on a small scale. So I always found that I was much more attracted by the microscope than the telescope. I was not overwhelmed in childhood by being told of remote stars which the sun never reached, any more than in manhood by being told of the empire on which the sun never set. I had no use for an empire that had no sunsets. But I was inspired and thrilled by looking through a little hole at a crystal like a pin's head, and seeing it change pattern and colour like a pygmy sunset.

I have already picked two quarrels with better men than myself, who were enthusiasts for childish romance, upon the reality of the romance of childhood. First, I disagree with them when they treat the infantile imagination as a sort of dream; whereas I remember it rather as a man dreaming might remember the world where he was awake. And second, I deny that children have suffered under a tyranny of moral tales. For I remember the time when it would have seemed the most hideous tyranny to take my moral tales away from me. And, in order to make this clear, I must contradict yet another common assumption in the romantic description of the dawn of life. The point is not very easy to explain; indeed, I have spent the greater part of my life in an unsuccessful attempt to explain it. Upon the cartloads of ill-constructed books in which I have completely failed to do so I have no desire to dwell. But perhaps, as a general definition, this might be useful; or, if not as a definition, at least a suggestion. From the first vaguely, and of late more and more clearly, I have felt that the world is conceiving liberty as something that merely works outwards. And I have always conceived it as something that works inwards.

The ordinary poetic description of the first dreams of life is a description of mere longing for larger and larger horizons. The imagination is supposed to work towards the infinite; though in that sense the infinite is the opposite of the imagination. For the imagination deals with an image, and an image is in its nature a thing that has an outline, and therefore a limit. Now I will maintain, paradoxical as it may seem, that the child does not desire merely to fall out of the window, or even to fly through the air or to be drowned in the sea. When he wishes to go to other places, they are still places, even if nobody has ever been there. But, in truth, the case is much stronger than that. It is plain on the face of the facts that the child is positively in love with limits. He uses his imagination to invent imaginary limits. The nurse and the governess have never told him that it is his moral duty to step on alternate paving-stones. He deliberately deprives this world of half its paving-stones, in order to exult in a challenge that he has offered to himself. I played that kind of game with myself all over the mats and boards and carpets of the house; and, at the risk of being detained during His Majesty's pleasure, I will admit that I often play it still. In that sense I have constantly tried to cut down the actual space at my disposal; to divide and subdivide, into these happy prisons, the house in which I was quite free to run wild.

I believe that there is in this psychological freak a truth without which the whole modern world is missing its main opportunity. If we look at the favourite nursery romances, or at least if we have the patience to look at them twice, we shall find that they all really support this view, even when they have largely been accepted as supporting the opposite view. The charm of Robinson Crusoe is not in the fact that he could find his way to a remote island, but in the fact that he could not find any way of getting away from it. It is that fact which gives an intensive interest and excitement to all the things that he had with him on the island; the axe and the parrot and the guns and the little hoard of grain. The tale of *Treasure Island* is not the record of a vague desire to go on a sea voyage for one's health. It ends where it began; and it began with Stevenson drawing a map of the island, with all its bays and capes cut out as clearly as fretwork. The eternal interest of the Noah's Ark, considered as a toy, consists in its complete suggestion of compactness and isolation; of creatures so comically remote and fantastic being all locked up in one box; as if Noah had been told to pack up the sun and moon with his luggage. In other words, it is exactly the same game that I have played myself, by piling all the things I wanted on a sofa, and imagining that the carpet around me was the surrounding sea.

This game of self-limitation is one of the secret pleasures of life. As it says in the little manuals about such sports, the game is played in several forms. One very good way of playing it is to look at the nearest bookcase and wonder whether you would find sufficient entertainment in that chance collection, even if you had no other books. But always it is dominated by this principle of division and restriction, which begins with the game played by the child with the paving-stones. But I dwell upon it here because it must be understood as something real and rooted, so far as I am concerned, in order that the other views I have offered about these things may make any sort of sense. If anybody chooses to say that I have founded all my social philosophy on the antics of a baby, I am quite satisfied to bow and smile.

I have no great hopes that my own private Utopia, the Utopia of subdivision and self-limitation, is likely to be rapidly established in the real world. I do not immediately expect that the landlord with five hundred acres will instantly cut it down to fifty acres, and stand in startled admiration of the fresh and pleasing shape, the entirely new and attractive map or outline of his domains. I hardly suppose that he will be romantically enraptured, all at once, at the discovery of the enchanted island that I have cut out for him, out of the dull and dreary sea of his solid landed estate. I doubt whether the simple kindly act of stealing half his books will drive him to reading the other half; I am not sure that the traditional childish present, of a little garden marked out in the middle of his large garden, will instantly change him to a little child. But I do know that great historic changes always begin at exactly the opposite end to the end the world is pursuing, and that the human search, so long turned outwards, will turn inwards very soon.

XXV. ON THE RENAISSANCE

In Rome a man feels suddenly the paradox of the Renaissance. It was a Christian miracle if it called up a Pagan god. It was in itself a Christian notion that, if the dead could return, they would not be shadows from Hades, but human beings from Heaven or Hell. But as a fact, of course, the god who rose again was not pagan. He could not be, since he was carved by Christians, even by bad and blasphemous Christians. Something that had not been in heathen antiquity had entered the very blood and bones of the human race; and it entered equally into the stone and clay of all that the human race could make. Without it, even the worst of men would now have felt suddenly cold and strange, like fishes, or, rather, like fossils. To be a Greek god was as impossible as to be a fossil, though both might be beautiful mouldings or even beautiful models in stone. To be completely heathen was no longer to be completely human.

The examples are obvious. Many people must have pointed out that Michelangelo was really more like Michael the Angel than Apollo the Archer. It was not for nothing that his very name is Hebrew and Greek as well as Italian. Every one must have noticed that there is, in some mysterious way, more colour in the monochrome marbles and bronzes of the Renaissance than in many of the cold, clay-like pigments that were called colours in the pagan houses of Pompeii. Even where the work is materially a matter of light and shade, it is not something put down in black and white: the light is richer and the shadow glows. Of course, a great part of the problem here is connected with modern religious controversies. Because modern pagans wanted to go back to paganism, in the sense of destroying Christianity, they said that the sixteenth-century artists wanted it too, though there was not one of them that would not have drawn a sword or dagger and destroyed the critic who told him that he wanted to destroy the Cross. Benvenuto Cellini would have been as prompt as Giotto; for the Christian Church is not made for good men, but for men.

The difficulty of history is that historians seldom see the simple things, or even the obvious things, because they are too simple and obvious. It is sometimes said of the pictures of the Renaissance artists, especially of the pictures of Rubens, that we ought to stand far back in order to take in the whole stupendous design, and not be annoyed because some detail is technically careless or emotionally coarse.

It is probably true of more than one Renaissance picture of the Resurrection; and it is certainly true of that general Resurrection that is called the Renaissance. There has been too much bickering over bits of the astonishing business; too much casuistry about whether this or that painter in this or that point surrendered to heathenism, or merely to human nature. The whole story consists of two staggering truths. First, that these men did really raise the dead. They did call up all heathenism, which might seem about as safe as calling up all hell. And, second, that they did really in a manner convert and christen the dead; that they did baptize all that bodily manifestation and materialization into the body of Christ. Even when it had been and was no more, it did become something that it had not been. They paraded before the world a wild hypothetical pageant of what old Greece and Rome would have been if they had not been pagan. To do this with any dead society is an amazing achievement. To copy the old body in any case is amazing; to copy the old body, and also put in a new soul, is amazing beyond praise beyond question, and certainly beyond quibbling. The fact is so familiar that it has ceased to amaze; the only chance of conveying it would be to take some fantastic parallel in modern and ancient things. We should be mildly surprised to hear that the English in Egypt had reconstructed for themselves the ancient Egyptian civilization; that all the proclamations of Lord Lloyd had been carved on obelisks in Egyptian hieroglyphics; that Lord Cromer had been preserved on the premises in the form of a mummy; or that Lord Kitchener at Cairo had religiously gone the round of worshipping a series of stuffed cats. But we should be surprised, with something less of mildness, if we were told that all this was done in such a way as to cause no embarrassment, or even amusement, to the English gentlemen who were doing it; and who managed to do it without the least sense that their code of manners was altered, or that their religion, when they had any, was suffering neglect. Just as it would be a remarkable thing for men to become ancient Egyptians and yet remain modern Englishmen, so it was a remarkable thing when these men became ancient Greeks and yet remained medieval Christians.

There are many morals to the story; but one must be manifest in the mere word I have used. If the medieval religion had really been such a silly superstition as some of its simpler enemies represent, it quite certainly *would* have been swallowed up for ever in such an earthquake of enlightenment as the great Renaissance. The fact that the vision of a superb and many-sided human culture did not disturb the fundamental ideas of these late medieval Christians has a simple explanation: that the ideas are true. The application of these true ideas in medieval times had been very much hampered by local ignorance and feudal prejudice. But the truths were so true that they would have survived, in really thinking men, through ten Renaissances and twenty Revivals of Learning. We see this vividly in the intensely intellectual character of the religious conviction in men like Michelangelo and even Leonardo da Vinci. Nobody knew better than they that Christianity is really wiser, and even wider, than Paganism; that Aquinas was not only better but broader than Aristotle. Not from such men came the clumsy denials of the deep dogmas of the Faith. Michelangelo was not the man to dispute that the truly divine humanity would be crucified; nor could Raphael be reckoned on for a breezy protest against the respect felt for the Madonna. But if the whole thing had been a dirty asceticism of the desert, the mere monkey tricks of the Manichees, it would have fallen like filthy rags from men who had seen the grace of the Greek athletes. If it had been only a worship of dolls with tinsel crowns, it would have looked a paltry and pygmy affair in the presence of the great head of Jupiter. But the real men of the Renaissance knew that, as a matter of fact, there was much more humanity in the rules for the brethren gathered by St. Francis than in the rules for the boys beaten before the altar of Diana; and that, as a matter of fact, the Church had a much more logical idea about the exact position of Jesus in Heaven than the heathens had ever had about the exact position of Jupiter on Olympus. It was the intellectual value of the creed that preserved it through any revolution of æsthetic values, just as it preserves it still amid the wildest changes in æsthetic taste to-day. Michelangelo went on being a Christian then, just as Mr. Eric Gill goes on being a Christian now, because a man may be original without being separated from the origins; and because a man may be able to think, even if he can also draw.

I would not be provocative, but I think this rather neglected truth is due to these great artists, when so many people imagine them to have been Pagans and some can even imagine them as Puritans. It seems clear to me that those despised medieval superstitions, suited only for barbarians like Dante and St. Francis, were exactly the ideas that did remain rooted in the most civilized centres of the world, when they were disputed in the more barbarous provinces. When we consider how exciting the destructive quest of the intellect really is (though it is generally people totally devoid of intellect who say so), it is really rather remarkable that there was comparatively so little of it in these great adventurers, who were devoted to the creative quest of the imagination. When we consider how wild they often were in the matter of morals (though it is generally the sort of moderns who have no morals at all who darkly denounce the immorality of these later men of the medieval decline), it is really rather remarkable that they kept as much as they did of the faith from which the morals grew—or ought to have grown. When we consider that it really is a fact (though the first fool in the street will tell you so) that scepticism had begun to appear here and there even among priests and bishops, it is really singular, upon the balance, that it had not appeared more among painters and sculptors. We may talk, as they sometimes may have talked, about reviving the gods of Greece. But Moses is Moses and David is David, and a Pagan would have stood puzzled before them.

XXVI. ON THE LAUREATESHIP

It is often said that the office of Poet Laureate is not fitted to our times. This is true; it is perhaps the most compact condemnation of our times. If we want to know exactly what is really lacking in current culture, we had better ask why it cannot support the idea of a real Poet Laureate. It is enough merely to look at the words which make up the title. Whenever it is suggested that some little modern man of letters, in a tail-coat and trousers, should be solemnly presented with a Crown of Laurel, everybody laughs, as if it were a joke. But it is not the laurel, but the little man, that is a joke. It is not the wreath of leaves, the lines of which are still as free and rhythmic and adapted to decoration as when they decorated a hundred marble monuments or golden frescoes; it is not the wreath that is ridiculous. It is the tail-coat and trousers; it is the Modern Man; it is the Spirit of Our Time, to which the Laureateship is, we have agreed, so unsuited. As is the Laurel to modern dress, so is the Laureateship to modern manners. Nobody sees anything silly in those leaves when they cluster round the hood of some bust of Dante. Nobody saw anything silly in them when, at the high moment of the medieval renaissance, they were bound about the brows of Petrarch. It was partly that the same scheme of decoration, more or less unconsciously, ran through the whole world of costume and ornament. It was much more because, in those dim and barbarous ages, people did not think it undignified to be dignified. They were so strangely constituted that they laughed at ugly things, and not only at beautiful things. A gentleman who wished to be stared at or admired dressed in purple and cloth of gold, trailing trappings that went in great curves like those of a comet or a cataract. With such fashions a crown was actually a crown; it crowned the edifice; it was a crest or culmination of lines rising to and demanding such a diadem. Nowadays, by the tradition of the nineteenth century, a gentleman dresses like a comic waiter in a third-rate farce, and is surprised that the bay-wreath looks grotesque on his head. But it is not the bay-wreath that looks grotesque.

That is a parable of the whole practical problem. And it always is a problem, whether it is worth while to keep the habit when it no longer makes the monk, or one small rag torn from the habit when the monk no longer knows how to make himself. The psychology of the Laureateship, dating as it does from the days when Petrarch was crowned with laurel, implies a number of things not now vivid to any very large number of people. It implies the notion of a *crowd* being excited but quite serious: like devotees before a sacrament or children before a fairy-play. There is still a certain kind of popular enthusiasm, but it is not an enthusiasm for enthusiasts. It might almost be called an affection for anti-enthusiasts; an affection for mockers and cynics and artists in the antic view of life. They might be as much thrilled by meeting Charlie Chaplin as any medieval Italians by meeting Petrarch. But though they might be cheering without jeering, they would be cheering somebody who jeers: who jeers admirably at himself and this wicked world. Nobody can expect that sort of popular artist to wear a laurel round his remarkable bowler hat. But it has been possible, and it will be possible again, for the public to rejoice seriously, and even solemnly. In those older days the very word "solemn" went with the word "joyous"; and "a high solemnity" was almost always an affair of dancing and junketing. A modern crowd would cheer the critical faculty, as in Mr. Chaplin; it would not cheer the creative faculty, as in Dante. And unless we keep the idea of a high solemnity, or public function of state, like the famous scene of the tribute to Petrarch, there is indeed little point in keeping merely an office and a name.

As we do not preserve the coronation it may seem idle to preserve the crown. Nevertheless, if there were a crown, I think I should preserve it—among the Crown Jewels. I should not attach any man to it, but leave it there and wait for better times.

For my part, though I have indulged in any amount of buffoonery, I regret the new and solitary pre-eminence of the buffoon. I regret the fact that the new popular hero must not be heroic as well as popular. He must not receive from the State a serious tribute for revealing a serious truth. When, for the moment, the most intelligent art is the most flippant art, it will mean a certain abdication of the old claims of the artist. But it may mean worse things than that. When people begin to ignore human dignity, it will not be long before they begin to ignore human rights. The pagan state, in which the artist is only a buffoon, will soon resemble the ancient pagan state in which he was only a slave. I am all for playing the goat; I am charitably disposed even to those enacting the funny dog; I have myself appeared more than once in public in the character of a performing elephant. But if we allow the Image of Man to fade away altogether in these animal antics, if it vanishes amid mere mockery and scepticism, the human being will find himself something very much worse than fair game. He may ultimately be tethered like the goat, or chained up like the dog, or ridden and prodded like the elephant.

The man who has exhibited himself—as in so much of modern prose and verse—in every attitude of abject and dishonourable ignominy will find it very much harder to spring up straight of a sudden and defend his honour, if his real intellectual and spiritual honour is attacked. Among the old ways of preserving this sense of honour was the system of honours; and, though most of them are now pretty thoroughly dishonoured, nobody suggests that the Poet Laureateship has been sold. Anyhow, among the wider ways of doing it was what may be called the Pageant of Poetry; the public acknowledgment of the Poet, "to whom the high gods gave of right their thunders and their laurels and their light."

XXVII. ON LIVING FOR POSTERITY

WE all remember the story of that excess of aspiration, in the sense of the use of aspirates, which led somebody to say of somebody, "If you give him a Hinch, he'll take a Hell." Some recent extensions of social liberty have made the accident of the last word sound strangely like an omen. But what strikes me as even more curious is this: that there are some people who are perpetually demanding an ell, but cannot be persuaded to accept an inch. They demand certain forms of social liberty in the large, but refuse them in the small, and especially in the solid. They are like people who should furiously demand a hundred head of cattle, and then flee in terror at the first appearance of a cow. Or they are like a king who should claim to rule the waves and be afraid to have a well or a pond in his own garden. The little more, and how little it is; and how lightly they will take the larger responsibility! The little less, and what miles they will run in order to be worlds away!

For instance, I read in any number of *New Leaders* and Labour weeklies, and all sorts of papers supposed to be both progressive and popular, that the working-classes will now take over the government of the country; that the majority of manual workers will have their proper proportional right to rule in all matters of education and humanitarian reform; that the poor will at last inherit the earth. But if I say that one workman is capable of deciding about the education of one child, that he has the right to select a certain school or resist a certain system, I shall have all those progressive papers roaring at me as a rotten reactionary. Why the workman should be clever enough to vote a curriculum for everybody else's children, but not clever enough to choose one for his own children, I cannot for the life of me imagine. If I say that a decent costermonger is to be trusted with a donkey, or a decent rat-catcher with a dog, I shall be denounced as an obstacle to humanitarian legislation. But there is no objection to trusting a crowd of costermongers and rat-catchers to decide about the humanitarian legislation. And what is true of these particular cases of proprietorship is true of the whole case of property. When the meek inherit the earth, it must only mean that the mob inherits the earth. It must not mean that the man inherits even the smallest portion of the earth. The mob is meek enough, certainly, when it is thus herded to its pastures by its sociological and educational pastors. It does not really mean that the many sheep, but that the few shepherds, will rule over all the meadows. And when the nomadic shepherd finds himself confronted with the static or domestic peasant, with the man who is actually ruling his own small meadow like a realm, there is always a collision and a sort of civil war in the country-side. In any case, the original paradox remains: that it was regarded as a simple thing that all the meadows should belong to all the men, but a frantic and fantastic thing that any man should own any meadow.

But there is another case that is even more curious. In the works of Mr. Wells, and all the typical Utopias and futuristic world-systems of recent times, it is incessantly and impressively repeated that we must live for the Future, for the Young, for the Rising Generation or the Babe Unborn. The traditional obligations of the past are nothing, and even the temporary contracts and compromises of the present are comparatively little; but we really do have a duty to the future generations. It is apparently the only duty that remains. While we are kicking our grandfather downstairs, we must take care to be very polite to our great-great-grandson, who is not yet present; and if a more enlightened ethic should ever justify us in painlessly poisoning our mother, it will be well to distract the attention by dreaming of some perfect Woman of the Future who may never need to be poisoned. These examples are quoted but lightly and from memory, but nobody will deny that current culture is in fact full of this notion of living for posterity. It is preached as a democratic doctrine in the democratic organs to which I have referred. But it is always the People as a whole that is to live for the Posterity as a whole.

But if we present precisely the same idea, in a present and practical form, it is called antiquated. Its practical form is called Marriage or the Family. It really does demand that a man and a woman should live largely for the next generation. It does demand that they should, to some extent, defer their personal amusements, such as divorce and dissipation, for the benefit of the next generation. And whenever we suggest that, a wail goes up about the wickedness and cruelty of depriving the poor dear parents of the innocent gaieties of divorce. How can a poor father get any real fun out of being divorced, if his enjoyment is to be dashed by a morbid memory of of the existence of his own son? Nay, can we even be certain that the mother will keep up her high standard of dancing all night and every night, if there is a new-born baby who (with curious taste) is crying for her all night long? When the problem of Posterity is presented in this practical form, poor old Posterity gets the knock pretty badly. The Present suddenly becomes much more important than the Future; and the rising generation is a mere drag on the risen generation, which intends to dance until it drops. In this case also, the new thinkers are only thinking of the general, and are afraid to think of the particular. Just as the Socialist must not confront a peasant with one concrete piece of land, so the Sociologist must not confront the parent with one concrete piece of Posterity. Otherwise the new parents will fly screaming, and in some cases adopt measures to ensure that there shall be next to no Posterity at all.

I grieve to say that I am not moved to a profound respect or admiration for this intellectual compromise. If the social idealist would take his inch I might be ready to trust him with his ell. If he could trust a poor man with the care of a cow or a cottage, or a common or garden child, I might believe he was sincere in wishing to trust all poor men with the destiny of all cottages and cows. As it is, I suspect that he is not going to trust that destiny to a democracy of poor men, but to an official or oligarch appointed to organize the poor men. Similarly, if the new social philosophies fervently encouraged people to think more about domesticity and less about divorce, I might believe that they really were preferring the future generation to their own. As it is, I think they want to procure all possible pleasures and amusements for their own, including the mild amusement of prophesying some Utopia that can only come long after they are dead. If their novels and newspapers were less filled with the sublime spiritual liberation of eloping with the chauffeur, and more filled with the duty and dignity of remaining with the baby, I might admit that their faces are set towards the Future and their souls full of the song of "A Good Time Coming." As it is, it seems to be an impatient and even pessimistic lyric about "A Good Time Now."

I am not at all pharisaical about these weaknesses considered as weaknesses, but I am rather bored with the pretence that they are strong with the strength of vigilant Watchers for the Dawn. And I am increasingly tired of the whole tone of that inverted idealism, which is terrified when told to make use of a single talent, but quite confident of its fitness to rule over ten cities. But I suspect, if I may describe the fashionable mood in terms of old-fashioned sentiment, that these people are only filling the Castle of Indolence with the Pleasures of Hope.

XXVIII. ON MR. SHAW'S PURITANISM

THERE was a time when I was asked, with quite a curious persistence, what I thought of Mr. Bernard Shaw and what he thought of Professor Einstein. It was especially in connexion with certain remarks about the nature of Great Men, and his reasons for limiting the list to some and excluding others. I had no difficulty at the time in answering that I thought of Mr. Bernard Shaw very much as I have always thought of him, and that I should have no difficulty in admitting him to my list of Great Men, though perhaps my list might be a little longer, and perhaps a little more liberal than his. I actually wrote a book about him in the ancient days, and I am happy to say that he reviewed it himself, with the typical opening: "This is the best book of criticism that I have yet produced." And what I said then is very much what I should say still: that there is no very fundamental antagonism between Mr. Bernard Shaw and myself except in one fact—that he is a Puritan and I am at least relatively a Pagan. It is true that I have become a Christian; but that is a thing that happened to quite a large number of Pagans. Only I never became a Puritan; and it seems to me that Mr. Shaw never became anything else.

Of course I know that there are a number of things to which his actual attitude would be merely negative or sceptical as compared with my own; but those things never affect me as real or ultimate disagreements, but merely as matters which he does not happen to have understood even sufficiently to disagree. They are part of a heritage of negation from the rebels of the nineteenth and eighteenth centuries: a rebellion that has become almost respectable with age. It is almost a mark of being behind the times to go on talking merely of traditional religion. What we have to deal with in the modern world is traditional irreligion. The period between Voltaire and Bernard Shaw is merely the period of the rise and decline of something that began as a joke and ended as a prejudice. Nobody will deny the wit of Shaw, any more than the wit of Voltaire; but these sceptical or negative notions are not even the jokes of Shaw: they are merely the prejudices of Shaw. The jokes of Shaw have been much more serious and socially useful things, and have been directed against things much more modern than ecclesiastical abuses which have long ago been more than sufficiently abused. They have been directed against the spiritual pride of physical science; against the Doctor's Dilemma and not merely against the Curate's Egg—a rather ancient egg which, after all, was always excellent in parts. They have been directed against the worldliness of San Francisco rather than the unworldliness of St. Francis. If he made fun of America, it was at least at the moment when America was being taken most seriously, and at the moment when the seriousness was certainly a form of snobbishness. I have never been disturbed by his disbelieving the things he does not understand, and I have always been delighted with his disbelieving the things he does understand: such as the Darwinian Theory or the Capitalist State. I should never be so stupid as to mistake Mr. Bernard Shaw for an irreligious man. He seems to me, in a rather special and vivid sense, to be a religious man. But there is always that deeper difference, and it is involved in the nature of the religion. And if I wanted a profound illustration of the difference that I mean, whether or no it is a difference I could explain, I could find it in a remark made in this discussion about Einstein and Great Men: a remark that may not seem to have anything to do with religion at all. Mr. Shaw is reported, and I apologize if he is misreported, as saying that he would hesitate to admit Napoleon into his select club of heroes; and that "it would have been better for the world if Napoleon had never lived." To which I answer that if Napoleon had never lived, then certainly Bernard Shaw never would have lived. At any rate, if Napoleon had not succeeded in being Napoleon, Shaw would not have succeeded in being Shaw.

For certainly if Napoleon, or some revolutionary soldier nearly as competent as Napoleon (there may have been one or two others who could have proved competent), had not appeared to save the French Revolution from the invading forces of the aristocracies and autocracies, reaction would have shut down on the first republican hopes like a trap of iron, and all the democratic dreams that have since filled the intellect and imagination would have been utterly and perhaps finally destroyed. All that we call the modern world, with all its good and evil, was made by Napoleon; at any rate was made possible by Napoleon. And among the various products of that original revolutionary expansion was the particular theory of reconstruction which we call Socialism. I will leave Mr. Shaw to decide whether that particular product is to be classed among the good or evil products of the French Revolution. But surely nobody with historical sense can doubt that all these modern ideals of revolutionary improvement, with the purpose of social justice or equality, date from the great idealistic movement at the end of the eighteenth century. Now I take it as certain that if the Revolution had not become militant, and been successfully defended by a man of military genius, it would have been easily crushed by the old oligarchies and despotic systems; and, having been easily crushed, would have been easily forgotten. There would have remained no legend of revolutionary victory; and therefore, alas for human nature, very little of revolutionary heroism. There would probably have remained, for centuries afterwards, not a gleam of revolutionary hope. I am merely stating the historical and especially the practical probabilities. I do not discuss here how far the balance would have been for evil or good. We should doubtless have avoided many annoying forms of anarchical nonsense such as still manage to live on the tradition of the triumph of France. We should have been less troubled with some mistaken mob movements, and some much more poisonous secret societies. But we should have missed some good things as well. We should have missed social reform as the serious preoccupation of the nineteenth century, we should have missed Socialism, and we should have missed Shaw.

Now I can heartily respect, and even sympathize with, some jolly old English Tory who still regards

Bonaparte as Boney. I can understand the genial reactionary, like Mr. Sapsea, who continues through all continental changes to drink the toast, "When the French come over, may we meet them at Dover." But I should hardly have thought of associating Mr. Sapsea with Mr. Shaw. And whatever may be the true story of the punishment of St. Helena, it seems rather hard on Napoleon that he should endure not only an eternal punishment, but a double punishment: one from all the reactionaries he defeated and the other from all the reformers he defended. It was the expansion of Napoleonic France that established everywhere the modern theories of civic right and equal opportunity; and the very name of that justice is the Code Napoleon. In the face of these facts, I naturally ask myself: Why does a man like Mr. Shaw hate Napoleon? Why does a man like Mr. Wells hate Napoleon? The only sincere answer is that it is the mark of the Nonconformist always to hate Napoleon.

It would take a long time to explain. A vague notion that a soldier is a naughty man; that he wears a cocked hat and sometimes even a cockade or a feather in it; that bodily fighting is always a blackguardly way of dealing with any position, however provocative; that soldiering is associated with canteens and cans; these and a thousand other things have created in the mind of the modern Puritan the mood of the modern Pacifist. We can all understand, that Napoleon himself would entirely understand, the higher sense in which it may be said that glory is vanity. But the Puritan always insists, not that glory is vanity, but that glory is infamy. He thinks this sort of action, this sort of ambition, not only the worst but the most horrible; he thinks there is no smell so foul as the smell of gunpowder. I think the smell of the hair-oil of hypocritical peace-mongering infinitely more offensive. Nobody will accuse Mr. Shaw's work of smelling like that; but there does come from it sometimes, suddenly, this strange stale smell of the Puritan; and it is then that I can answer our old question: Do We Agree?

XXIX. ON THE TRUTH OF LEGENDS

I HAVE known all my life what is called the conflict between romance and realism, and I have always found that it was the realists who were romancing. I have found, in a fashion too curious to be a coincidence, that the romances were generally real after all. For instance, everybody knows how a boy is told that his boyish day-dreams are only day-dreams, and will not long survive in daylight; that his picturesque figures of the Red Indian or the Jolly Tar are only painted and pasteboard figures out of a toy-theatre, or melodramatic personalities out of a penny dreadful. It is taken for granted that he will begin by believing in them and end by disbelieving in them. In a number of solid historical cases, I myself began rather early to disbelieve them, and have come eventually to believe them. I seriously think that the popular sentiment that created those characters was often a tradition of truth, where the pedantic cynicism which destroyed them was often a much more deliberate perversion of truth. The tradition may have come down rather loosely and vaguely, through a long line of nurses and grandmothers. But the nurses and grandmothers were not paid to tell lies, and they did therefore, to a considerable and very valuable extent, tell the truth. The critics and historians *were* paid to tell lies; though they may not have put the truth to themselves in quite so crude a fashion. They were academic officials of a certain academic system; achieving a fame which depended upon a fashion; successful or unsuccessful, according to the power of a theory; suiting themselves, consciously or unconsciously, to a certain school; and, when all is said, living by receiving salaries or selling books. They had not the disinterestedness or detachment of gossip. They were not merely mentioning the things they remembered, but remembering only the things they were supposed to mention. Their minds had formed a mechanical habit of recording only the things that were suited to the records, and writing only the records that were suited to the official record office. Some of them were stark liars; some of them, which is much more strange and uncanny, were honest men. But they were, at best, men telling untrue stories in the interest of the truth, or what they believed to be the truth. They were not ordinary people telling true stories, merely as stories that were curious because they were true. It is all the difference between the chronicler and the historian. And the difference is that the chronicler sometimes told fables; whereas the historian never tells fables, but only falsehoods. However this may be, I have known a curious number of cases in which mere sentimental gossip surrounded my childhood, and serious historical scholarship surrounded my manhood; and the sentimental gossip was right.

For instance, it was sentimental gossip that Mary Queen of Scots was very badly treated; or that Charles the First was to be pitied or even admired. I remember loving both the historical characters as legends, and then learning afterwards that the legends were entirely legendary. The historical realists of that time told me that the attraction of Mary Queen of Scots was merely that she was much prettier than Queen Elizabeth. They told me that the charm of the Cavalier consisted only in his wearing more picturesque clothes than the Puritan. Those who told me this were often learned, and those who had left me with the earlier impression were often ignorant; and I myself was unfathomably ignorant. I therefore believed what they told me; I proceeded to believe, to believe blindly, credulously, and in hopeless intellectual servitude; to believe in the much more fabulous fable, in the legend of the learned. I believed much more seriously—that is, much more superstitiously—in the school text-book than I had believed in the old wives' tale. But the old wife was an old wife by the normal process of becoming a wife and growing old, and she employed the normal habit of talking to children about her childhood. But the schoolmaster was a professional schoolmaster; the schoolmaster was tied to his school; the schoolmaster was as much under discipline as the schoolboy.

In the case of Mary Queen of Scots or Charles the First, which I have mentioned, it is, of course, perfectly true that there are two sides to the story. What I complain of in the schoolmaster is that he always taught only one side of the story. So, it may be said, did the nursery story-teller. But her story was a story in the literary sense of a legend. His story was a story in the nursery sense of a lie. It was a lie in the very real sense that he was not merely reporting what he had heard, but very carefully selecting from what he had read. Of course, as I say, it is perfectly true that there is a case for the Calvinists who opposed Mary Stuart, or the later Calvinists who opposed Charles Stuart. Of course, it is arguable that Mary Stuart killed her husband, or that Charles Stuart broke his word. Of course, it is arguable that it was better for England that the Whigs should turn it into an aristocracy than that the Stuarts should turn it into an autocracy.

But that is not the point. The point is that the

ignorant legend was much more true, as far as it went, than the learned legend as far as it went. To paint a portrait of Mary Queen of Scots as a lovely, unhappy, charming, and cultured lady, brutally baited by barbarous Puritans and tragically martyred by a jealous Tudor tyrant, is a process of portraiture very far from complete; but it is in its way true, even when it is not complete. To paint a portrait of Queen Elizabeth as a prophetic lioness of Protestantism, upholding the Huguenots out of mere love of the Holy Scriptures, and brandishing a Bible to cow all the Papists of the world, is not a process of portraiture true but incomplete; it is simply completely untrue. It is contradicted by every fact in Elizabeth's history, from her continuous invalidism or ill-health to her continuous intrigues about marrying Catholic princes. And the first truth, or half-truth, was a truth of tradition. The second lie, and complete lie, was a lie of scholarship. Similarly, the popular legend was not lying about the kind of atmosphere, or even the kind of glamour, surrounding King Charles and the Cavaliers. It may have been little more than a romance; the legend really recorded little more than a romance; but it was the real romance. It was not false when it represented the Cavalier with his goblet lifted and his sword drawn; ready to drink to the King, ready to die for the King. For thousands of such men did actually drink to him and did actually die for him. It was not romancing to say that the Royalist had a romantic loyalty. It would not have been romancing to say that the Puritan had a religious loyalty. He had a loyalty to the letter of Scripture, to the logic of Calvin, to the awful duty of spreading true religion.

But my schoolmasters did not tell me that the Puritan stood for religious loyalty, which is true. They told me that he stood for religious liberty, which is a lie of that mountainous and monstrous order which ignorant traditionalists call a Whopper. They were not concerned, like the traditionalists, with gathering up, however lazily, the loose fragments of a truth. They were concerned with covering up most carefully the most accidental glimpses of the truth; with so picking their words and arranging their sentences that no suspicion of the main truth of the matter should really penetrate to the reader. It is amazing to consider how carefully and how successfully they did cover up a truth so obvious and so enormous. There is, for instance, the perfectly simple fact, written in large letters across the history of two reigns and practically two revolutions, that the last Stuarts tried to establish religious toleration and the Puritans tried to prevent religious toleration. It would seem as impossible to hide so huge and simple an historic fact as to hide the fact that Nelson fought for England and Napoleon for France. Yet men like Macaulay and Green really did manage to hide it from a whole rising generation, the generation with which I myself originally rose. But, fortunately, I had learned some truths in my childhood before I began to learn lies in my boyhood. And all my subsequent knowledge has led me to prefer the pictures which honestly professed to be picturesque to the plans and diagrams which dishonestly pretended to be accurate.

XXX. ON EXPERIENCE

It will be remarked that Experience, which was once claimed by the aged, is now claimed exclusively by the young. There used to be a system of morals and metaphysics that was specially known as the Experience Philosophy; but those who advanced it were grim rationalists and utilitarians who were already old in years, or, more commonly, old before their time. We all know that Experience now stands rather for the philosophy of those who claim to be young long after their time. But they preach something that may, in a sense, be called an Experience Philosophy, though some of the experiences seem to me the reverse of philosophical. So far as I can make it out, it consists of two dogmas: first, that there is no such thing as right or wrong; and secondly, that they themselves have a right to experience. How they manage to have any rights if there is no such thing as right I do not know; nor do they. But perhaps the philosophy was best summed up in a phrase I saw recently in a very interesting and important American magazine, quoted from one of the more wild and fanciful of the American critics. I have not the text before me, but the substance of the remark was this. The critic demanded indignantly to know how many ordinary American novelists had any Experiences outside those of earning their bread, pottering about in a farm or a frame-house, helping to mind the baby, and so on. The question struck me as striking at the very root of all the rot and corruption and imbecility of the times.

On the face of it, of course, the whole question is rather a joke; only that these gay pleasure-seekers and revellers in the joy of life have seldom been known to see a joke. We might politely inquire exactly how much Experience is needed to equip a novelist to write novels? How many marks does he get for being vamped or for being intoxicated; and which are the particular discreditable acts by which he can get credits? How many liaisons give him this singular rank as a literary liaison officer; and how many double lives does it take to constitute Life? Is it only after his fourth divorce that he may write his first novel? For my part, I do not see why the same principle should not be applied to all the other Ten Commandments as well as to that particular Commandment. It should surely be obvious that, if love affairs are necessary to the writing of this particular sort of love story, then it follows that crime is necessary to the writing of any kind of crime story. I have myself made arrangements (on paper) for no fewer than fifty-two murders in my time; they took the form of short stories; and I shall expose myself to the withering contempt of the young sages of Experience when I confess that I am not really a murderer, and have never yet committed an actual murder. And what about all the other forms of criminal Experience? Must a writer be a forger, and manufacture other men's names before he is allowed to make his own? Must there be a journalistic apprenticeship in picking pockets as well as in picking brains; and have we to look to the establishment of an Academy of Anarchy, with the power of conferring degrees? Novelists might proudly print after their names the letters indicating the degrees they had taken; such as F.Y.B., meaning "Five Years for Burglary," or T.N.H., for "Twice Nearly Hanged." Altogether it may be said that writers do not rob, but it may be fortunate that robbers do not write. It is possible that the wild and wicked criminal might, after all, make almost as good a novelist as the novelist.

It would also be easy enough to attack the fallacy upon the facts. Everybody who has any real experience knows that good writing would not necessarily come from people with many experiences. Some of the art which is closest to life has been produced under marked limitations of living. Its prestige has generally lasted longer than the splash made by sensational social figures. Jane Austen has already survived George Sand. Even the most modern critic, if he is really a critic, will admit that Jane Austen is really realistic, in a sense in which George Sand is only romantic. She was, indeed, a flaming, fashionable figure created entirely by the Romantic Movement; but Jane Austen did not belong to any movement; she does not move, but she stays. And, though I do not agree with the too common depreciation of Byron, it is true that all his somewhat excessive Experience, in the new or juvenile sense, has not prevented people feeling him to be the very reverse of realistic, and in some ways strangely unreal.

But there is, of course, a much deeper objection to the whole of this new sort of Experience Philosophy, which is quite sufficiently exposed in the very examples I quoted from the magazine. There are certainly all sorts of experiences, some great and some small. But the small ones are those which the critic imagines to be great, and the great ones are those that he contemptuously dismisses as small. There are no more universal affairs than those which he imagines to be little and local. There are no events more tremendous than those which he regards as trivial. There are no experiences more exciting than those which he dully imagines to be dull. To take his own example, a literary man who cannot see that a baby is marvellous could not see that anything was marvellous. He has certainly no earthly logical reason for regarding a movie vamp as marvellous. The movie vamp is only what happens to the baby when it goes wrong; but, from a really imaginative and intellectual standpoint, there is nothing marvellous about either of them, except what is already marvellous in the mere existence of the baby. But this sort of moralist or immoralist has a queer, half-baked prejudice to the effect that there is no good in anything until it has gone bad. It is supposed to be a part of Experience for the woman to be a vamp, but not for the woman to be a mother; although it stares us all in the face, as a stark fact of common sense, that child-bearing really is an experience, and a highly realistic experience, while the other sort of experiment may not really be an experience at all. It may be in the exact sense mere play-acting; and, as the game is now played, the main preoccupation is to prevent its ending with an addition to the cast of characters. Whatever happens, it must not be the means of bringing on the scene a new, breathing, thinking, conscious creature like a baby. That would not be Life.

Now, if there is one thing of which I have been certain since my boyhood, and grow more certain as

I advance in age, it is that nothing is poetical if plain daylight is not poetical; and no monster should amaze us if the normal man does not amaze. All this talk of waiting for experiences in order to write is simply a confession of incapacity to experience anything. It is a confession of never having felt the big facts in such experiences as babyhood and the baby. A paralytic of this deaf-and-dumb description imagines he can be healed in strange waters or after strange wanderings; and announces himself ready to drink poisons, that they may stimulate him like drugs. But it is futile for him to suppose that this sort of quackery will teach him how to be a writer, for he has been from the first admittedly blind to everything that is worth writing about. He will find nothing in the wilderness but the broken shards or ruins of what should have been sacred in his own home; and if he can really make nothing of the second he will certainly make nothing of the first. The whole theory rests on a ridiculous confusion by which it is supposed that certain primary principles or relations will become interesting when they are damaged, but are bound to be depressing when they are intact. None of those who are perpetually suggesting this view ever states it thus plainly; for they are incapable of making plain statements, just as they are incapable of feeling plain things. But the point they have to prove, if they really want their Experience Philosophy accepted by those who do not care for catchwords, is that the high perils, pleasures, and creative joys of life do not occur on the high road of life, but only in certain crooked and rambling by-paths made entirely by people who have lost their way. As yet they have not even begun to prove it; and in any case, and in every sense, it could be disproved by a baby.

XXXI. ON SIGHTSEEING

I HAVE often done my best to consider, in various aspects, what is really the matter with Sightseeing. Or rather, I hope, I have done my best to consider what is the matter with me, when I find myself faintly fatigued by Sightseeing. For it is always wiser to consider not so much why a thing is not enjoyable, as why we ourselves do not enjoy it. In the case of Sightseeing, I have only got so far as to be quite certain that the fault is not in the Sights and is not in the Sightseers. This would seem to drive the speculative philosopher back upon the dreadful and shocking conclusion that the fault is entirely in me. But, before accepting so destructive a deduction, I think there are some further modifications to be made and some further distinctions to be drawn.

The mere fact that a mob is going to see a monument ought not in itself to depress any imaginative and sympathetic mind. On the contrary, such a mind ought to perceive that there is something of the same mystery or majesty in the mob as in the monument. It is a weakness to fail in feeling that a statue standing on a pedestal above a street, the statue of a hero, carved by an artist, for the honour and glory of a city, is, so far as it goes, a marvellous and impressive work of man. But it is far more of a weakness to fail in feeling that a hundred statues walking about the street, alive with the miracle of a mysterious vitality, are a marvellous and impressive work of God. In so far as that ultimate argument affects the matter, the sightseer might almost as well travel to see the sightseers as to see the sights. There are, of course, vulgar and repulsive sightseers. There are, for that matter, vulgar and repulsive statues. But this cannot be a complete excuse for my own lamentable coldness; for I have felt it creeping over me in the presence of the most earnest and refined sightseers, engaged in inspecting the most classical and correct statues. Indeed (if I must make the disgraceful confession in the interests of intellectual discovery), I will own that I have felt this mysterious wave of weariness pass over me rather *more* often when the elegant and distinguished Archdeacon was explaining the tombs to the Guild of Golden Thoughts than when an ordinary shouting showman was showing them to a jolly rabble of trippers with beer bottles and concertinas. I am very much troubled with this unnatural insensibility of mind; and I have made many attempts, none of them quite successful, to trace my mental malady to its origin. But I am not sure that some hint of the truth may not be found in the first popular example that I gave—the example of a statue standing in a street.

Now, men have stuck up statues in streets as part of the general and ancient instinct of popular monumental art, which they exhibited in erecting pillars, building pyramids, making monoliths and obelisks, and such things, from the beginning of the world. And the conception may be broadly stated thus—that this sort of sight was meant for two different kinds of sightseers. First, the monument was meant to be seen accidentally; it was actually set up purposely in order to be seen accidentally. In other words, a striking tower on a hill, an arresting statue on a pedestal, a remarkable relief over an archway, or any other piece of public art, was intended for the traveller, and even especially for the chance traveller. It was meant for the passer-by, perhaps in the hope that he would not merely pass by; perhaps in the hope that he would pause, and possibly even meditate. But he would be meditating not only on something that he had never seen before, but on something that he had never expected to see. The statue would almost spring out upon him like a stage brigand. The archway would arrest him and almost bar his path like a barricade. He would suddenly see the high tower like a sort of signal; like a rocket suddenly sent up to convey a message, and almost a warning. This is the way in which many popular monuments have been seen; and this, some may agree with me in thinking, is pretty much the best way to see them. No man will ever forget the sights he really saw when he was not a sightseer. Every man remembers the thing that struck him like the thunderbolt of an instant, though it had stood there waiting for him as the memorial of an æon. But, whether or no this be the best way of treating popular memorials, it is not the only way, and certainly has not been the only popular way. Historic relics, as a whole, have been treated differently in history as a whole. But, in history as a whole, the other way of seeing such sights was not what we commonly call sightseeing.

We might put the point this way: that the two ways of visiting the statue or the shrine were the way of the Traveller and the way of the Pilgrim. But the way of the Pilgrim almost always involved the way of the Pilgrimage. It was a ritual or ceremonial way: the way of a procession which had indeed come to see that shrine, but had not come to see anything else. The pilgrim does not feel, as the tourist does often quite naturally feel, that he has had his tour interrupted by something that does not happen to interest him. The pilgrimage must interest him, or he would never have been a pilgrim. He knows exactly what he wants to do; and, what is perhaps even more valuable, he knows for certain when he has done it. He cannot be dragged on from one thing to another; from one thing that interests him mildly to another thing that bores him stiff. He has undertaken a certain expedition with a certain logical end: an end both in the sense of a purpose and in the sense of a termination. For a certain mystical reason of his own he wanted to visit a certain monument or shrine; and, now he has visited it, he is free to visit the nearest public-house or any other place he pleases.

But all this is altered, because we have passed from the age of monuments to the age of museums. We have been afflicted with the modern idea of collecting all sorts of totally different things, with totally different types of interest, including a good many of no apparent interest at all, and stuffing them all into one building, that the stranger may stray among a hundred distracting monuments or the pilgrim be lost among a hundred hostile shrines. When the traveller saw the statue of the hero, he did not see written on the pedestal: "This way to the Collection of Tropical Fungi," in which he possibly felt no interest at all. When the pilgrim found his way to the shrine, he did not find that the priest was eagerly waving him on to a glass case filled with the specimens of the local earthworms. Fungi and earthworms may be, and indeed are, exceedingly interesting things in themselves; but they are not things which men seek in the same mood which sends them to look at the statues of heroes or the shrines of saints. With the establishment of that entirely modern thing, the Museum, we have a new conception, which, like so many modern conceptions, is based on a blunder in psychology and a blindness to the true interests of culture. The Museum is not meant either for the wanderer to see by accident or for the pilgrim to see with awe. It is meant for the mere slave of a routine of self-education to stuff himself with every sort of incongruous intellectual food in one indigestible meal. It is meant for the mere Sightseer, the man who must see all the sights.

Of course, I am only speaking of this kind of sight as it affects this kind of sightseer. I do not deny that museums and galleries and other collections serve a more serious purpose for specialists who can select special things. But the modern popular practice of which I complain is bad, not because it is popular, but because it is modern. It was not made by any of the ancestral instincts of mankind; either the instinct that erected the crucifix by the wayside to arrest the wayfarer, or the instinct that erected the crucifix in the cathedral to be the goal of the worshipper. It is not a product of popular imagination, but of what is called popular education; the cold and compulsory culture which is not, and never will be, popular.

XXXII. ON CONDIMENTS AND CONDUCT

I HAVE always wondered why there is no New Religion forbidding the use of salt and pepper; not to mention the more monstrous case of mustard. I cannot understand how it is that no Moral Movement, no deeper stirring of social consciousness, no wave of higher citizenship and devotion to the ideal of Service, has appeared to start some people interfering with other people in the use of condiments—of all those pungent luxuries with which an effete and self-indulgent civilization has hitherto complicated its meals; taking salt with eggs, mustard with beef, pepper with mutton, and all sorts of strange, unnatural sauces with everything else. Surely there ought to be a Crusade against these things, since a Crusade is now commonly held to mean an attack upon some habit of Christian civilization. Very little would be needed to set the Puritans, who are above all Manicheans, denouncing these things exactly as they now denounce beer or tobacco, and are, indeed, already beginning to denounce coffee and tea. In contradiction of the advertisement recently so common, we should see the town plastered with the words "Joint the No-Mustard Club." By a slight emendation of Scripture (which is nothing to the devout Puritan) we should be told that the salt which has *not* lost its savour is fit only to be cast forth and trampled under foot of men.

Such a Puritan version of salt in the Gospel would be far less impudent than the Puritan version of wine in the Gospel. In a hundred ways we should be assured of the corrupting and degrading character of these condiments; and terrible stories would be told of ruined families weltering in anchovy sauce as if in gore, or darker stories of that darker drug, the sauce that bears the name of Worcester. I could myself, on the spur of the moment, easily make up all sorts of arguments and illustrations as convincing against condiments as others are against convivial liquors. I could point out that the old proverb about taking strange stories "with a grain of salt" was itself an evidence of the connexion between strange substances and strange delusions, and bring out the result that salt is really a sort of opium. I could point out that the very fact of mustard being hot in the mouth is analogous to the old phrase about ginger being hot in the mouth, which has come to be a sort of euphemism for vice or violent self-indulgence. I could point out that pepper is actually used by criminals as something to fling in the faces of their pursuers, to blind and choke them. So that the pepper-pot takes its place in the police museum as being both a weapon of crime and an instrument of torture.

It seems as sensible to argue that some criminals make a bad use of pepper as to argue that some drunkards make a bad use of port wine. For those who sneer at tobacco may be expected, in the same sense, to sniff at snuff, and presumably to snivel over pepper, for a great part of their moral eloquence consists of sniffing and snivelling. Nothing is needed, for most of their moral movements, but a sort of gesture of priggish repugnance and small-minded superiority; and it would be just as easy for a moralist to make that sort of face over a jar of pickles as over a pot of porter. A curious mixture of the snobbish sneering of the middle classes against the working classes, with the more morbid snarling of the invalid against the healthy man, has made a large number of things that are simply common appear merely coarse. So perhaps we may look forward to fresh purifications of society, purging it of all the poisons of pepper and salt and sauce, and reducing it to plain living by this remarkable course of high thinking. Vinegar would be forbidden by the teetotallers, because of its wicked past when it was wine. Mustard would arouse a similar Moslem or Judaic fury, because it is generally eaten with ham.

The equality of the sexes, in eternal ethics, would be asserted by saying that there shall be no sauce, either for the goose or for the gander.

By the way, though the point is a parenthesis, what a remarkable anticipation that proverb is of modern muddle-headedness about the sexes! It is, in fact, often used, in the sex controversy, as a metaphor meaning that one sex or sort must in all things be treated like the other. But nothing could be more unlucky than the metaphor, whatever we may think of the moral. If there is one thing to which this argument of sameness or assimilation does not apply, it is to the question of sex in connexion with the solemn question of supper. Suppose the sauce is egg-sauce; am I to wait patiently for eggs from the cock, as an alternative to eggs from the hen? I will not eat cow-beef if I can help it, merely on the ground that what is mustard for the bull is mustard for the cow. Nor will I look for milk from the bull, however much I may recognize the general necessity of milk rather than mustard. It is something rather typical of the way these things are treated that people should express their view in proverbs rather than principles. The scientific course is obviously to begin by clearing up the question of what is the real difference between a goose and a gander, and then pointing out that it does not affect the question of sauce, though it may very much affect the question of something else. But this laborious method is very unpopular with a generation which thinks that self-assertion is a complete substitute for self-criticism, or, indeed, for any other sort of criticism. In that world we are well acquainted with the sort of goose who possesses very little except sauce.

But this, as I have said, is merely a remark in brackets, in the course of other remarks about other heresies. We are chiefly concerned with the heresy of the Manichees, which has already expressed itself in the denunciation of wine and even tobacco, and might just as well express itself, I would suggest, in the denunciation of mustard or even salt. For the essence of that idea is that every pleasure as such is suspect; or that, unless a thing can be specially shown to be morally good, it is most probable that it is morally bad. There is no real defence of a luxury except to prove that it is a necessity. Now, it would be much easier to argue, in certain cases, that wine is a necessity than that vinegar is a necessity. There are certain practical good effects sometimes produced by the tobacco plant which are very seldom produced by the pepper plant. The enemies of these drinks or drugs, as they would call them, may think that the evil of them enormously outweighs the good; so enormously as to justify their extinction as pure evils.

But they could not deny that the drug is a drug; in the double sense in which a drug is normally regarded as good and evil. They could not deny that such a thing is a drug, both in the sense of something consumed by a drug-fiend and of something sold by a druggist. They may think it unwise to use it for an immediate remedy, but it is used for an immediate remedy. Smoking has been known to serve for some time as a substitute for eating, and a cigarette does sometimes soothe the nerves of a neurotic. Brandy and champagne are constantly administered in illness, except among rank and raving lunatics. But I have seldom heard of an invalid leaping to life after a draught of anchovy sauce; or of anybody eating pepper for days on end; or of people in hysterics being quieted with pickles. If it ever comes to the old Manichean controversy about useless luxuries, I think it will be harder to defend the condiments than to defend the stimulants, or even the intoxicants. I am presuming that such Puritans will carry out the moral philosophy that is really at the back of their minds; it does not affect me, for I have quite a different moral philosophy at the back of my mind. It would occupy too much space to expound it here, and I have often enough expounded it elsewhere. But it might be indicated by saying that there is a truth behind the joke of the man who said:

"Give us the luxuries of life and we will dispense with the necessities"; and the truth can be more soberly stated by saying that, in one sense, human beings are not even completely human, until they are civilized.

XXXIII. ON OPTIMISM AND SCEPTICISM

I SUPPOSE people will go on till the crack of doom saying (as somebody said the other day) that Browning expressed the opinion that God is in His heaven and therefore all is right with the world. I could mention a number of other opinions that Browning expressed, in exactly the same method and degree. I could point out that Browning said, in his gay and careless fashion: "Which is the poison to poison her, prithee?" doubtless referring to Mrs. Browning. I could note that Browning observed, when brooding on his own immediate course of action: "Or there's Satan . . . one might venture pledge one's soul to him." It will occur to every reader of the poet that he observed on a celebrated occasion: "Lo! lieth flat and loveth Setebos," presumably prostrating himself upon the carpet in Wimpole Street. It will also be recalled that Browning, after confessing to various frauds and lies, virulently cursed the patron to whom he had confessed them, saying: "I only wish I dared burn down the house and spoil your sniggering." If these incidents in the life of the poet cause any surprise, it may be well to explain that they are, in fact, incidents in the lives of his characters; and so is the much-quoted phrase about all being "right with the world." It is not a remark made by Browning, but a remark made by Pippa in the dramatic work by Browning. Even those who know that the remark occurs in a lyric do not always know that the lyric occurs in a drama. It has therefore a double right to be considered dramatic. It is a remark made by a particularly dramatic character on a particular dramatic occasion, and, above all, for a particular dramatic reason. And the reason is not a desire to show that all is right with the world, but to bring out in sharp contrast the fact that there is a great deal very wrong with it.

So far as that is concerned, the facts (as everybody knows, or ought to know) are these. The idea of the play called "Pippa Passes" is that a very poor girl, on her one solitary holiday, goes singing through the world in a state of perfect innocence and therefore of perfect gaiety. In doing so she crosses various human groups who are the very reverse of innocent or gay, each of whom is at some crisis of crime or sin or sorrow. In each case, as she passes, she sings a song, of which the innocence tingles through them in the form of irony. She passes by a house where a wife has just seduced her lover into murdering her husband, and, by way of the last violence of contrast, sings a little song about the morning being so beautiful that all seems to be right with the world. One would have thought it would have occurred to most readers that Browning was not very likely to think that assassination and adultery were actually examples of the rightness of the world. The point was not, of course, that all was right with the world, but that all was right with Pippa, because she had kept herself unspotted from the world.

It is perhaps worth while to mention this queer old blunder about Browning, and what is called his optimism, because we have since seen a great deal of optimism that is very much less reasonable than his. Browning did, indeed, believe that God is in His heaven, though the mere fact of the song of Pippa would not prove that he did. He did believe in God; and, curiously enough, he is not entirely alone in that, and in some quarters the curious superstition is even spreading anew. But he did not believe that all was right with the world, in the sense that there is no wickedness, madness, or misery in it; his works possibly contain a larger and more varied assortment of blackguards, miscreants, maniacs, and miserably deluded people than those of any writer of his time. If you had gone to Robert Browning with the definite and deliberate doctrine, "There is no pain or evil," he would certainly have classed you among the maniacs. He would very probably have written a long, ingenious, and partly incomprehensible poem about you in blank verse, but your portrait would be even less pleasing than that of Sludge the Medium or Caliban. Yet the same people who go on quoting poor Pippa's little song as a proof that Browning was absurdly optimistic, have lived to see the preaching of an optimism that he would have thought utterly absurd.

Elsewhere, I recently remarked that the new optimism, though it expresses itself in commerce and journalism, and especially in advertisement, probably has, like everything else, its roots in religion. Its essence, or at least its extreme expression, is to be found in what is called Christian Science. Anyhow, it does what Browning and the old optimists never dreamed of doing—it denies the actual reality of evil in experience. At any rate, it maintains that by ignoring evil we can expel it from experience. It is this which is the last phase of philosophy popular in America, and to some extent in England. And it has gone very much further than the human holiday cheerfulness of the poor Italian work-girl in Browning's poem. For one thing, the American optimist especially insists that the work-girl shall sing optimistically about her work, as well as about her holiday. She must sing a new song of optimism even as she labours; to the effect that the Boss is in his office and all is right with the world.

Curiously enough, all this new sort of optimism can be traced back to a sort of scepticism which is very much nearer to pessimism. It may almost, in a sense, be traced back to a great pessimist. Nobody ever accused Hamlet, Prince of Denmark, as depicted by Shakespeare, of being an American optimist. Nobody ever reproached Hamlet with being a hustler, a go-getter, a business man with plenty of pep and sand, an active and animated member of Rotary. But these busy business men are all acting on a philosophical principle drawn from Hamlet, and thoroughly typical of Hamlet: "There's nothing either good or bad, but thinking makes it so." That is the original germ of Christian Science, but also the original germ of Business Optimism. I believe that those mystics, the members of the American business clubs, go about with large labels or buttons on their coats inscribed with the words "Trade is Good." The savage who thinks he can hurt a man by writing his name in the dust could hardly be more superstitious. But, anyhow, for good or evil, whether it be superstition or science, it marks a belief in the power of words over things, or, if you will, of ideas over realities, which goes far beyond the dreams of the older optimists. Some of this sect of optimists, I believe, recently held a sort of religious ceremony in which they cursed an old woman dressed up as Mrs. Pessimism, and bowed down before a queen called Mrs. Optimism. That does not seem very far from lying flat and loving Setebos.

I protested a short time ago against the abominable slander of suggesting that most Americans are like these people. Most Americans laugh at them, even more derisively and destructively than we do. America may be a country of strange sects, but it is also a country of almost continuous satire on strange sects. Nobody needs to add anything to the satire of Mark Twain and some more recent writers on people like Mrs. Eddy. But it is worthy of remark that America has given birth, among many other strange sects, to this strange sect of the commercial optimist, who may perhaps be best defined as the Unrealist. The creed is perhaps the corruption of many good things, of the ancient American hope and pioneering courage gone wild. But, as there seems a tendency, even in England, to boost this mere religion of boosting, an Englishman may be allowed to protest that it is preposterously unsuited to England and is not really respected even in America. Christian Science may or may not start with the assumption that God is in His heaven and all is right with the world; it is a subject for a respectful debate with Christian Scientists. But Christianity emphatically began with the assumptions that God has come on earth because all is wrong with the world; and from those two things the whole Christian theory proceeds.

XXXIV. ON THOUGHTS IN CANADA

I NEED not say what any normal Englishman feels, or ought to feel, when he sails up the St. Lawrence, under the high trophies on the Heights of Abraham, and I have never affected any new abnormality about such feeling. My thoughts, when I was there, went back in one flash to the little town in the hills of Kent where I had been but a few weeks before: the little town where James Wolfe was born and where his statue still stands, sword in hand, in a romantic but not inappropriate swagger. For Wolfe, who was one of the most interesting of English heroes, was himself a flat contradiction to the vulgar and prosaic version of English heroism. It is strange that people should ever have talked of the English as if they must be heavy, stupid, and brutal. It is still more astounding that they should ever have been proud of being heavy, stupid, and brutal. It would be nothing to be proud of; and, in fact, it is not even there for them to be ashamed of. In historical fact, it is a very recent affectation: a mixture of the bad fashion of copying Prussia and the growth of a modern materialism which is solemn about sports because it has no other rites to solemnize.

Englishmen were more sportive about sports in the days of General James Wolfe; and the battle of the Heights of Abraham was won on the village green, with very rotten old bats and stumps. And the men who represented England, in the days when her Empire was really an adventure, were the very opposite of the sort of stuck pigs who are called strong, silent men. Nelson and Wolfe, the two noblest names of England's action by land and sea, were both of them men of exactly the opposite kind: sensitive, poetical, even cursed with what is called the artistic temperament. Nelson suffered from something which is even worse than the artistic temperament—sea-sickness. Wolfe was of the slight and high-strung sort, and owed nothing of his bravery to brutality. He was himself, I believe, an artist with the pencil, of considerable felicity and talent: he was devoted to books, and, whether he did or did not quote Gray's *Elegy* as he sailed up the St. Lawrence to death and glory, it was exactly the sort of thing he would have done. But there is another aspect of the fine culture and dignity in Wolfe and the earlier English heroes which seems to me to teach a sad but salutary lesson. As I sailed past Quebec, I was told by a fellow-traveller a thing I had never heard before, which moved me very much. With all our talk of globe-trotting and sightseeing, it seems to me that some of the finest sights of the globe are neglected or not appreciated. It was only by such a casual stranger that I was once told, what I hope is the truth, that on the mountain range between two South American Republics, which had made peace with each other, there stands a colossal figure of Christ; apparently one of the largest, and surely one of the most impressive, statues in the world. But it stands, if it does stand, alone and enormous upon the mountains. Somewhat in the same way I had seen many tributes to Wolfe, of a worthy or unworthy sort. I had seen him in patriotic posters, figuring side by side with people whom he would have intensely disliked, such as Cecil Rhodes. But it was only this chance information which informed me that a monument has been set up on that high place to Wolfe and Montcalm together, with a fine Latin inscription saying that fate gave to them the same death and the same honour.

And when I thought of that worthy commemoration, of those two great and gallant soldiers, it occurred to me that they were, in truth, nearer together, even in their lifetime, than most of their kindred are to-day. There were real differences, of course; Montcalm was a noble and Wolfe a man of the middle classes, risen by merit; but their notion of the manners, the code of honour, and the necessary information of a gentleman would have been very much the same. Neither would have thought it odd for a soldier to go about quoting poetry; both would have thought it quite ordinary and obvious to be quoting Horace. I fancy there was a far wider division, at the beginning of the Great War, between French and Foch. The older generals were nearer together as enemies than the modern generals were as allies. By which I do not mean to refer to any of the quarrels about quarrels, the reports of rivalries or irritations in the higher command, which occur in all wars, and can easily occur between fellow-countrymen. I mean that the whole make-up of the mind of a man like Foch was more exclusively French, and more puzzling to a man who was exclusively English, than was a great continental noble to a scholarly Englishman like Wolfe. The Latin of Horace was a link between two eighteenth-century gentlemen, whether French or English. The Latin of the Mass, as heard by a French soldier, is not a link with the Latin of the Latin grammar as vaguely remembered by an English soldier.

We are perpetually being told to-day that nations are drawing nearer to each other; Mr. Wells is supposed to be engaged in an Open Conspiracy in the matter; I can only say that, if it is open, it is not at all obvious. I grieve to say that I gravely doubt it. I fear that the French and English, at this moment, understand each other a great deal less than they did not only when they were allies in the Great War, but even when they were enemies in the older and lesser wars. Indeed, the farther we go back the closer the French and English come together. The Black Prince and Bertrand Duguesclin were even more capable of understanding each other than Montcalm and Wolfe. That would not, of course, have prevented them from killing each other, which was all in the game. But they would have agreed much more about the rules of the game, and especially about the rules of the killing. The truth is, of course, that France and England were very nearly one nation in the Middle Ages; at least, in the early Middle Ages. The English kings especially were always trying to make them one nation; but then it must be remembered that, in a sense, even the English kings were French kings.

Now, I do not wish myself to make England and France one nation; my views on that subject are the same as those energetically advanced by St. Joan of Arc. But I do think it a fitting subject for sober and prayerful consideration, whether with invocations to St. George or St. Denis, to St. Joan the fighter or St. Francis the peacemaker, that these two great Western nations have steadily drifted further and further apart through the centuries, and are now so very far apart as they are. The national division is really dangerous when it cuts across all other differences, and is really much deeper than they. There have always been strong hatreds against special types or tendencies, such as much of the medieval world felt against the Moslem or much of the modern world feels against the Bolshevist. But, though men may hate Russia because of Bolshevism, they do not hate France because of Republicanism or Roman Catholicism, or any one definable intellectual idea.

The ordinary Englishman does not understand either the French Republican or the French Royalist; he is equally mystified by the French atheist and the French Catholic. The English Radical cannot comprehend the French Radical; the Englishman who is most loyal to his own monarch is utterly ignorant of the French case for a return to monarchy. Yet France is still what she always was, the intellectual focus and creative crater of Christendom; the place where the ideas are hammered out and tested which are to build or to destroy a world. Those who do not understand what is happening in Paris are dangerously ignorant of what will soon be happening everywhere; for all Frenchmen are Radicals in the sense of going to the roots of things, and none more Radical than the Royalist. And it seems to me a very menacing and perilous thing that we have lost, so much as we have, that one flash of the ancient Western understanding which shone for an instant on the marching armies of the Marne.

XXXV. ON THE BAD WORD FOR GUILD

It is a very old controversial custom to give a dog a bad name, which is generally the more learned scientific name for a cat. It is then, of course, a comparatively easy and natural matter to nail him up as a bat or a barn-door owl. Such fantasies of logic are the commonplaces of controversial history. The most usual form of the process, as we all know, is to fix some person with a definite label, and then proceed to deduce everything from the label and nothing from the person. I have experienced this in my own small way often enough. Somebody will write: "Mr. Chesterton is a medievalist; and he is therefore quite justified (from his own benighted standpoint) in indulging as he does, in the sport of tearing out the teeth of Jews, burning hundreds of human beings alive, and perpetually seeking for the Philosopher's Stone." But I never said I was a medievalist; and I have only the very vaguest idea of what it would mean. But I have a very vivid and definite idea of what I mean. And what I mean does not involve providing free dentistry for Jews; though indeed there is only one doubtful tale of King John doing to one Jew what it is now considered highly hygienic to do to everybody. Nor does it include seeking for the Philosopher's Stone; though it might involve seeking, somewhat wearily, for the Philosopher. The simple truth, which some people seem to find it so difficult to understand or to believe, is that what a reasonable man believes in is not this or that *period,* with all its ideas, good or bad, but in certain ideas that may happen to have been present in one period and relatively absent from another period. But nothing can convince his critics that he does not think in terms of hats and coats and caps and feathers and jerkins and hooded robes. Nothing will convince them that he thinks in terms of thought.

A very good working example is in the word Guild. As a matter of fact, it is the moderns and not the medievals who use the word in a romantic and irrational way. Anything in the world may be called a Guild nowadays: a society for picking up orange-peel may be the Guild of the Golden Gleaners; or a company of pierrots performing at Margate and Ramsgate may be the Guild of the Ghostly Guitars; or a movement for muzzling cats as well as dogs may be a Guild for Equal Rights for Four-Footed Friends. For whenever *we,* who are accused of this mysterious medievalism, happen to say a word in favour of the Guild idea, nobody seems to imagine for a moment that it is really an idea. Now, as a matter of fact, it is an idea, and in that sense nothing less or more than an idea. It is an economic and ethical theory for the construction of certain parts of society; and it has nothing in the world to do with the romance or ritual externals or picturesque costume of that society. To say that you believe in Guilds is like saying that you believe in Trusts, or in State Ownership, or in Syndicalism, or in any other definite way of managing certain matters of trade and employment and exchange. In my opinion, the Middle Ages were fortunate in having begun to develop industry in this way. But the Middle Ages were extremely unfortunate in many other ways; and not least in being ultimately unable to develop it. But if anybody says that I merely behold, as in a dream, ideal craftsmen in coloured garments carving exquisite masterpieces, or happy apprentices dancing round the maypole or distributing the Christmas ale, then he is a hundred miles away from the point at issue. The case for the Guild has nothing to do with the romance of medievalism; nothing whatever.

The theory of a Guild, as distinct from Socialism as generally defined, and Capitalism as at present practised, is simply this. The men working in a particular trade remain independent tradesmen; in the sense that they are independent and therefore up to a point competitive. Each is working for himself, with his own capital or machinery, and in that sense each is working against the others. But each has entered into an agreement with the others, that he will not compete past a certain point or work against the others in certain unfair and forbidden ways. In other words, there is a competition, but it is a deliberately limited competition; or, if you will, an artificially limited competition. The object is perfectly simple: that it should remain a competition, and not merely turn into a combine. Capitalist competition, which started avowedly as unlimited competition, has only been running freely for about a hundred years, and everywhere it has turned into a combine. I use the word combine as a polite convention; for, of course, we all know that it involves no equality of combination. The true story of the thing is that when all the shops are let loose to compete anyhow and everywhere, by any method good or bad, one shop swallows all the rest. To speak more rightly and worthily, one man swallows all the rest. It is very often, by the nature of the competition, the worst shop and the worst man.

Now the Guild method is no more medieval than it is modern, in so far as it is a principle apart from time. The best proof is that it does still exist in a practical profession with which we are all acquainted. The Doctor, the ordinary general practitioner, whom most of us know and to whom many of us owe our lives, is a typical example of the member of a Guild. He is not a Socialist official; he is not a State servant; he is an example of private enterprise. That is to say, he owns his own lancet and stethoscope; he has to buy his own practice; he does in a certain degree compete with the men of his own trade. But he is forbidden to compete with them by certain methods; he is forbidden to drive another doctor out of his practice by certain expedients of self-assertion or self-advertisement; he has to observe towards his fellow-doctor a certain respect and consideration. He has to do this because he has joined a Guild or confraternity, which exists for the maintenance of the members of his profession as a whole. Its definite and deliberate policy is to keep all the doctors in existence, as far as possible, and *prevent* one of them destroying all the rest. Once it is admitted that a man may use any methods of advancement and advertisement, the chances are that about twenty honest doctors would be swallowed up by one quack. We know this is what has happened in journalism and in commerce, and in any number of other things.

It is also to be noted that the other side of the old Guild idea, which balances this idea of preserving the small man in independence, the idea of testing him as to his claims to such independence, is also true of the modern doctor, as of the medieval Master. It is often regretted that Trade Unions do not insist, as did the Guilds, on a standard of workmanship and finish. They cannot do so under modern conditions, because they exist to contend with another and specially modern evil. But it is quite true that, before the Guild protected a man from unfair competition, it examined him in the mastery of his craft; and all that obviously corresponds to modern medical examinations and medical degrees. Now a man may quite reasonably disapprove of this system, just as I, in my own opinion, quite reasonably approve of it. He may say quite truly that it has evils of its own. He may say quite tenably that in his view those evils outweigh the good. But his attitude is neither true nor tenable if he pretends that the case for this social system is a mass of romantic rubbish about the perfect beauty of the Middle Ages. He is simply making a fool of himself when he talks of the method by which all the most modern surgery is accomplished and all the most novel medical theories advanced as if it were a mere fantastic dream of bringing back falconry and tilting-armour; or as if nobody could trust Sir Stanley Hewett or Sir Thomas Horder without wanting to wave a pennon or wear a tabard.

XXXVI. ON SOPHISTICATION

SOME are complaining that the rising generation is sophisticated; and it is true that some members of it are too sophisticated even to believe in sophistry. They believe in nothing; which I suppose is one way of returning to simplicity. The golden age of the sophists was somewhere about the last half of the nineteenth century. The Victorians were lectured and led a dance by any number of sophists; but that was because the Victorians were unsophisticated. They believed the most crazy paradoxes; as that it was more practical not to be logical; which is like saying that we should make sure of having a chain and not bother whether it consists of missing links. They believed that men must always have the same morality, though they had a new religion or no religion; that is, they said that what was done now for a definite reason would be done indefinitely for no reason. Those sturdy Saxon ideas were all sophistries; but that did not mean that the sturdy Saxon who accepted them was necessarily a sophist. What I think has really happened, in the case of the more sophisticated youth of to-day, is that they have become sceptical of everything, including scepticism.

And though two blacks do not make a white, it has sometimes been known, in grammar and philosophy, that two negatives make a positive. So that the sophisticated youth who has seen through the sophistical old men, may even yet see something worth seeing.

But there is one way in which the young seem to me not sophistical but very simple; and there is one type or section of them that is sufficiently simple to be called silly. A great deal of the current cult of pleasure, of luxury, of liberty in love, and all the rest of it, appears to me to be perfectly childish; and childish in the literal sense that it is greedy without any grasp of consequences. I read novels and poems in which the seeker after pleasure simply goes on saying, over and over again: "I must have Happiness. I must have Life. I must have Love. Why do you reproach me because I cannot live without passing from ecstasy to ecstasy?" This seems to me about as simple as the speech of a savage who should say: "I must have Gin. I like Gin. I like more and more Gin. Why will you not instantly provide me with a hundred bottles of Gin?" It does not seem to require much intellectual strenuousness to say this. It is, like other simple things, quite true as far as it goes. But in the matter of connected thought and the sense of consequence it does not go very far. Gin does make a man happy; up to a point more gin will make him more happy; but even more gin will make him many other things as well. By a succession of phases not contemplated by the philosopher in his first phase, it will make him first drunk, then dead drunk, and then dead to the world, and then very possibly dead altogether. That also seems to be a simple truth, requiring no great subtlety; but the savage cannot see it, and the sex novelist cannot see it. He cannot see, what nearly everybody in history has hitherto seen, that there are certain laws and limits to the mind, as there are certain laws and limits to the body. There is such a thing as concentration; there is such a thing as contrast; there is such a thing as proportion; there is emphatically such a thing as boredom. Above all, there is such a thing as a contradiction in terms; and it is a contradiction in terms to have every moment a crisis, every event an escapade, every fact an exception, every person an eccentric, every day a holiday, or society an endless Saturnalia. If people try to do that, they will find it dull; just as certainly as, if they drink unlimited gin, we shall find them drunk. If you do literally paint the town red, you will not be able to use it as a background, either to the red flag of Bolshevism or the red flower of a blameful life. If you do literally go on till all is blue, you will not be able to distinguish the special and delicate blueness even of the decadents' blue roses and blue wine. These are laws of the mind, analogous to laws of the eye. And the laws of the eye are not altered by everybody putting on the same sort of horned spectacles, that each of them may look separate and distinguished.

But there is one particular form of this modern simplicity that has always puzzled me very much. I mean the way in which those who dislike certain old things, such as war or discipline or various forms of danger, talk about ending them without asking how they begin. They always assume an association between these things, which none of us particularly likes, and other things which they particularly dislike. They say, for instance, that kings or capitalists, or some other privileged class, have invented flags and frontiers, that we may be drilled to defend them with guns and bayonets. They do not seem to see that they might need the guns and bayonets even if they were not defending the frontiers and flags. They might need them if they were defending anything. They might need them if they were defending their own ideal social state. And, as a matter of historical fact, they always do find that they need them to defend the very state that was invented to do away with them. But I am very much puzzled by the childlike simplicity with which idealists walk into this trap. It was true to some extent of the eighteenth century republicans, though those old republicans were a hundred times more intelligent than most of our twentieth century sceptics. Still, some of those charming philosophical gentlemen, of the age of Rousseau and Voltaire, did tend to talk as if the Natural Man would find it easy to break the sword when once he had broken the sceptre. They did talk as if nobody but kings would ever want cannons, and battles could only arise out of the dynastic ambitions of despotic states. We all know the ironic but very inspiring sequel. The sequel was that the Republic was born amid the roar of its own cannons; that it could only manage to survive by fighting battle after battle with merciless valour and armies growing more military every day; until the final fury of that militancy sent forth the greatest warrior of the world.

In the face of this example, the Bolshevists did exactly the same. In face even of the Bolshevist example, our own English Communists are doing exactly the same. The Russian revolutionists also began by being pacifists. They also set all their hopes on merely dissolving the discipline of the despotic armies. They also seem never to have reflected that they would want to have revolutionist armies, if only to fight the despotic armies. And of course, in an incredibly short period of time, they found out the very simple fact that revolutionists cannot be pacifists. They may set up what they call a peaceful republic, but they have to make up their minds what to do, if other people will not leave it in peace.

Suppose the Utopian has founded his Utopia, and another country makes war on Utopia. What, when all is said and done, is he to do? Is he to allow his perfect state (or what he is so simple as to think his perfect state) to be destroyed and disappear? Or is he to defend it by the only weapons that will defend it? One would think this dilemma was so staringly obvious that anybody must have seen it from the very first. That dilemma has nothing in the world to do with crowns or sceptres or capitalism or private property. Let anybody imagine any sort of simplified society, and I can imagine it being attacked. That fact seems simple enough for an infant to see. Yet I have read scores of young pacifist poets and prophets who could not see it. That is an example of what I mean by a sort of simplicity almost more exasperating than sophistry. That is a case of the same sort of simplicity as supposing that cocktails can be unlimited or gate-crashing continue when there are no gates.

XXXVII. ON DRESS AND DECORUM

THE newspapers very frequently, perhaps too frequently, describe to us the Victorian Girl, who was always covered with blushes and confusion. On the other hand, the Modern Girl has more and more of the confusion, as she has less and less of the blushes. Confusion of thought, confusion of phraseology, confusion of philosophy, deepen and darken upon her as she advances into what she regards as the daylight, or the sunlight of the Sun Cure. She and all her world seem to have got into a hopeless chaos about deciding the real principles of convention and civilization. Whatever theory we may hold, we find that she holds all the theories and none of the theories; that her theories contradict each other and cancel out. The ordinary argument in the newspapers, on the subject of Dress and Decorum, for instance, is a hash of half a hundred inconsistent philosophies. It may be worth while that some of them should be sorted out, before there are too many of them to be counted.

To begin with, there is the great contradiction that the modern person pretends to be at once too innocent and too sophisticated. First he says that certain sins are so remote and repulsive that only a low-minded spy would suspect their existence. Then he goes on to say that these sins are not so very bad, even if they exist. He shouts at the top of his voice: "To the pure in heart all things are pure"; and then goes on to explain that there is really no such thing as purity. He calls the moralist a Puritan, as the most withering of all terms of abuse; which is very amusing to some of us, who remember how recently we were called upon to admire the Puritanism of the *Mayflower* and the execution of Charles the First, and to pardon the massacre of Wexford and the witch-smelling of Salem merely because they were Puritan. He describes any decent citizen as Nosey Parker or (with a touch of fierce anti-feminism) as Mrs. Grundy; all with the object of suggesting that nobody but a person with an impure imagination could see anything but spotless purity in the pagan habits of our time.

Well, all that is applicable enough, when there is really anybody to apply it to. I have myself protested against Puritanism and Parkerism and the sour vigilance that would arrest the amusements of the populace. I entirely agree that it is disgusting to be nosey about anything that is normal; such as dancing or swimming, considered in themselves. My position on that point is what it has always been, and my position is perfectly clear. But the position of the New Pagan is not in the least clear. For the New Pagan attempts to maintain, at the same time, that the real violation of Christian morals is unimportant to the Pagan moralist. But in that case, how can it be wrong for the Christian moralist to accuse the Pagan moralist? The Christian cannot be merely morbid in saying that sin is involved, if the Pagan says that sin is irrelevant even if it is involved. I may be mad if I accuse my friend Smith of stealing the spoons, when he is a respectable person with the ordinary respect for private property. But I cannot be morbidly and insanely malicious when I say he might steal the spoons, if he says himself that he *will* steal the spoons. I may call it being a thief, and he may call it being a Class-conscious Communist Expropriator. But it is absurd to pretend that property does not matter, and then to be indignant at the charge of thinking it does not matter. It is equally absurd to deny propriety as to deny property, and then to say that only a fiend would suspect you of disregarding the property or propriety that you deny.

This is an obvious example of the modern muddle, but it is an annoying one. Whether certain acts are wicked or no we will debate when the statement is clearly made to us. But a thing cannot be so wicked that it is insane to suggest it, and so innocent that it is blameless to do it. There are, however, a large number of other confusions which any clear-thinking man can see in the modern commentary. We talk about the pagan philosophy; but the trouble with our own pagans is that they have no philosophy. We talk, by a sort of habit, about Modern Thought, forgetting the familiar fact that moderns do not think. They only feel, and that is why they are so much stronger in fiction than in facts; why their novels are so much better than their newspapers. The current comment on all these things is not even pagan; it is the queerest sort of patchwork of pagan and purely Christian ideas.

For instance, somebody is sure to say in the debate about Decorum: "Is not the human body beautiful?" To which somebody a little more sensible will be quite entitled to answer "No." If he is a Scot, and therefore a Socratic philosopher, he will be entitled to answer the question with a question, and say: "Is the hippopotamus beautiful?" The hippopotamus is certainly natural, even if he looks unnatural. He is certainly naked, and accepts no regulations about bathing-tents or bathing-costumes. But the mere fact that he is natural does not make us, in the ordinary sense, admit that he is beautiful. Personally, for my own part, I think he is beautiful; but then, I have a Gothic taste for the grotesque, nourished upon gargoyles. I know what I mean by saying that gargoyles may be beautiful. But the modern materialists do not know what they mean by saying that men must be beautiful.

All that talk about the divinity and dignity of the human body is stolen from theology, and is quite meaningless without theology. It dates from the Garden of Eden, and the idea (which I happen to hold firmly) that God created Man in His own image. But, if you remove that religious idea, there is no more sense in saying that every human being is lovely than in saying that every hippopotamus is lovely. It is a matter of taste; and many of us, after watching a sufficient number of human beings at Brighton, might prefer the hippopotamus.

The old atheists had a theory of life, that could be stated as a connected train of thought. The old theologians had a theory of life, that could be stated as a connected train of thought. But the moderns who call themselves Pagans have no connected theory that can be stated at all. Their view of life is a hotch-potch of human and superhuman and subhuman ideas, collected everywhere and connected nowhere. The modern muddler likes to think he is the Superman; likes to think he is the image of God; likes to think as he pleases; but prefers not to think at all. If he had the humility to behave like a beast, we should at least be free from the obligation to regard him as a god. We should not be bound to admit that every beast is beautiful; having religious doubts, perhaps, about the hippopotamus or the hornbill. If he would clearly and consistently aspire to beauty, we might ask him to add to it a little dignity. But in fact he has returned to chaos, where there is no asking, nor is there any answer. If man comes out of chaos, by blind evolution or merely groping growth, there is no more sense in calling his body noble than in calling any lump of fungus or cactus noble. If it is noble, it is so by some patent of nobility; and nobility is conferred by a King. But I advise such writers to defer the study of the Body and begin to employ the Mind.

XXXVIII. ON ALGERNON CHARLES SWINBURNE

I

Most modern titles and slogans have to say the precise opposite of what they mean, for the sake of brevity. Sometimes the organizers are so sincere as to explain this immediately afterwards; and use the sub-title to prove that the title is not true. A little while ago a series of short stories appeared, proclaiming in its editorial title that each author had chosen his best story. But the editor, who evidently suffered from intelligence (and it does sometimes entail suffering) was perfectly well aware that no sane author would say that any one story was absolutely and in all aspects the best; indeed, a sane author is more likely to be hag-ridden with the horrid memory of the worst. So the editor put in a note to explain his own title, which he said was necessary, because it was so much shorter. It is true that the phrase "My Best Story" is very much shorter than the more accurate phrase, "I think this story is one of the relatively few by which I might possibly consent that people should judge my general intelligence, such as it is." It is also true that the phrase, "This story is utter trash," is very much shorter than the phrase, "This story is not, fairly considered, quite absolute and utter trash." But they do not, to say the least of it, mean the same thing. And selecting the shorter would be unwise, even in a publicity expert.

A rather similar problem arose about a recent selection of English essays, made and introduced by the late Lord Birkenhead; it was a very good selection, and it was not alone in suffering from the particular problem. In large letters on the title-page it had to bear the title of "The Hundred Best English Essays"; and in the very first words of the introduction Lord Birkenhead very sensibly said that there could not possibly be any such thing as "The Hundred Best English Essays." He proceeded, in a very frank and sympathetic manner, to explain that it was not only impossible for anybody to do anything except make a reasonable collection of very good essays, but that he (for his part) had practically put in all the essays simply because he liked them. I really do not know what else any one can do with essays but like them—except, of course, if one has such darker reactions, dislike them. Of all forms of literature they are perhaps the least to be fitted into the old standards of judgment, by which it was in some sense possible to legislate for the drama or the ode. But, anyhow, there is something a little amusing about the claims of publicity and business requiring us to reverse all that we mean, in order to get anybody to listen to what we say. There is something comic about sacrificing everything to the headline, and letting it insist that the article should stand on its head.

I did not mention this book of essays, however, with the purpose of passing in review all its essays, still less the nature of the essay. I have to thank the compiler for bringing back many good things I may have missed or forgotten; but the one which especially caught my eye and concerns my pen is an excellent study by a critic lately dead of a poet whom he knew well and of whom he writes admirably. I refer to the essay on Swinburne by Sir Edmund Gosse. It contains any amount of matter upon which others could pronounce with much more authority than I. I only met Swinburne once; and though I met Gosse a great many times, I would never claim to have got past the guard of that polished rapier any more than anybody else. I had one letter from him about Stevenson, which I count one of the great honours of my life; for the rest, I was only one of a crowd of younger men to whom he was both ironical and kind. But there is something in the general and very vivid picture of Swinburne which he presents, which makes me inclined to linger perhaps belatedly on that name; and on the poetry which, as poetry, was as straight as a singing arrow; but, considered as philosophy, has always puzzled me very much. In other words, if we consider the target of the arrow, we find that there is nothing to consider; it is not even so clear a concentric scheme as a labyrinth; it is rather a labyrinth without a centre.

In plain words, after reading Gosse's essay again, I asked myself: "What on earth did Swinburne mean? Or did he mean anything?" It is easy enough after reading some of the poems, especially the later, longer and generally lesser poems, to say that he did not mean anything; that he was simply a musician gone wrong; a lunatic with something singing in his head; a creature throbbing with suppressed dancing; a creature who could not help foaming at the mouth with flowers and flames and blood and blossoms and the sea. But it is not easy, after reading Gosse's essay, to deny that he did in some way take something seriously; and something not himself, if his contemporaries doubted whether it was something for making righteousness. He did take counsel with Landor and Hugo as if they were grave gods making a world of justice or right reason. He did seem really to believe that some Utopia depended on the success of Cavour or the failure of Louis Bonaparte. But exactly how he connected it in his own mind with the queer licentious pessimism, like the last debauch of a suicide, which fills his other verses, I cannot make out; nor how he supposed that anything, even a Utopia, could be made of such flames and foamings. Surely he was not hoping for a republic in which all the citizens should be free to bite each other. Surely the hounds of spring, so hopefully upon winter's traces, were not all of them frothing at the mouth like mad dogs?

Yet it is his taste in virtue rather than his taste in vice that puzzles me. In the worst and most world-famous of all his lines he wrote something about the raptures and roses of vice and the lilies and languors of virtue. The obvious thing to say is that he cannot have known much about virtue, if he thought it was languid. But, to do him justice, his own appeals to public virtue were anything but languid. When talking of his own favourite type, which used to be called Republican Virtue, he seems to have understood all that Roman dignity and decency which he tore to rags in his ravings about sex. He used another nonsensical tag about somebody being "noble and nude and antique." So good a scholar ought to have known that, in the real world of the antique, a noble would never have desired to be nude. He would have regarded it as the mark, not of a noble, but a slave. In reality Swinburne knew all this; indeed one could hardly be a friend of so very ancient a Roman as Landor without knowing it.

Then, again, the Pagan philosophy he pitted against Christianity is a mass of such inconsistencies. In *Songs Before Sunrise* he offers Pantheism as the religion of the revolution. Pantheism may or may not be a good creed for a philosopher; Pantheism is certainly in one sense a very good creed for a Pagan philosopher. But Pantheism is a hopeless creed for a revolutionist. If all things are equally divine, then the tyrant and the bigot are as divine as the tribune and the truth-seeker. In "Hertha" he imagines the universe as a vast tree, out of which all things in turn bud and bloom; and then takes refuge in the miserable metaphor of saying that "creeds" are merely worms that have got into the bark—the devil knows how. If all things are equally unfolded from one natural root, the worms of oppression are as natural as the flowers of freedom. If they came otherwise, then the universe is not universal; and the worm in the tree of nature is as theological as the snake in the tree of knowledge. There might indeed be a war of spring sproutings against dead leaves or decayed fruit; but that only means that each is equally good in its season. And what is the good of a revolutionary creed that cannot denounce a tyrant in his season of strength? I believe that this folly of making

Pantheism the creed of liberals has a great deal to do with the decline of liberal politics and the reactions against it to-day. Hertha, explaining (at some length) that she is everything, remarks, if I remember right:

> I the mark that is missed
> And the arrows that miss.

It will strike a thoughtful mind that such arrows are rather likely to miss. William Tell will not fight well for Freedom, if he thinks that he and his bow and the target and the tyrant are all the same thing.

II

When I say that Swinburne's praise of virtue puzzles me more than his praise of vice, I do not (I may respectfully explain) mean that my natural taste in villainy makes me regard it as normal to be a villain, or that my brain reels with mystification when I contemplate any proved and public act of decency. I do not mean that crime is second nature to me, or that I set myself like a sleuth to track down a man and discover why he is not a murderer. What I mean is this: that in the case of Swinburne the loose poetry was really loose. It was flowing, both in form and spirit, and rather after the fashion of the flowing of tears. It was self-expression, but it was not self-assertion; and it certainly was not any other kind of assertion, like the assertion of a definite heresy or sophistry. In so far as there was something indefensible, he was not defending it. He was, perhaps, describing it, and it may be a bad thing that such things should be described; but such things are not in any case the materials of a moral or political system. Such hysterical, half-involuntary confession is not uncommon in literature, especially when (as is almost certainly the case with Swinburne) the literary man is confessing what he has never done. Anyhow, over the whole of this department of the poet's work there is a spirit of appealing and almost engaging despair, a pessimism about the impotence of man. He does not pretend that the pagan gods are good; he only confesses that they are strong—or, in other words, that he is weak. What puzzled me was how he really reconciled this part of his work with the other part, in which he professed to see a new hope for men in the virile and universal Republic, in which men should become heroes in becoming citizens. There is hardly a hopeful line in *Songs Before Sunrise* that could not be answered with a hopeless line from *Poems and Ballads*. Perhaps the most musical and magical verse in "Dolores" is that in open glorification of "the implacable beautiful tyrant"; and what is the use, after that, of denouncing all tyrants as implacable? What is the good of remaining rigid with horror of Napoleon, when you have flung yourself in a lyric ecstasy before Nero? What is the use of saying that you bring seed by night to sow, that men to come may reap and eat by day, when it is apparently so very easy for anybody at any moment to be tired of "what may come hereafter to men that sow and reap"? What is the sense of shouting about crowning man as the king of all things, if "the crown of his life, as it closes, is darkness; the fruit thereof dust"?

Nevertheless, there is another sense in which I would not dwell harshly upon the looser type of verse, as part of the real problem of this strange personality. I say that the poet in the poem does not defend himself. The poet in prose was less wise, and defended himself indefensibly. I do not care so much as Gosse did for the ranting and railing prose in which Swinburne accused his critics of being unjust to him; nevertheless, I think that they were unjust to him. I do not mean that he was right; but I do mean that they were wrong. The critics were wrong in the worst way in which a critic can be wrong about a poem: in being wrong about the point of it. The poem may contain a great deal that is pointless or beside the point; it may contain a great deal that is lawless and shameless and really at enmity with morals—in which case I am so old-fashioned as to think that it ought to be denounced and even destroyed as such. But even in condemning it we must condemn its point; and to condemn its point we must comprehend its point. We must understand what the man has really said, and not hang him as a heretic for saying something he never said. Now much of the wilder part of *Poems and Ballads* is not meant to describe merely a rush towards the antics of animal love, but a reaction from the tragedy of true love. The poet, in a morbid mood of mockery, is bitterly professing (we might say pretending) to prefer the gutter to the palaces of ideal enchantment, from which he has been cast forth by fickleness or pride. It is not a nice state of mind. It is a very nasty state of mind; but it is that state of mind and no other, and not the state of one who always preferred gutters because he was a gutter-snipe. To put the point shortly, we cannot understand the poem called "Dolores" without reading it side by side with the poem called "The Triumph of Time." For instance, I have condemned, as every sane critic has condemned, all that hydrophobiac nonsense of Swinburne about people "biting" each other. But it is not quite fair, even to that infernal nonsense, to read it without remembering the verse to which it in some sense leads up, and which is the true inner burden of the poem:

> In yesterday's reach and to-morrow's,
> Out of sight though they lie of to-day,
> There have been and there yet shall be sorrows
> That smite not and bite not in play.
> The life and the love thou despisest,
> These hurt us indeed, and in vain—
> O wise among women, and wisest,
> Our Lady of Pain.

I do not think the heartless woman is the wisest woman; I venture to doubt whether Swinburne thought so. But Swinburne did say so; and this is what he said; and what he meant was that the pains of a nobler love are so much more terrible that perhaps the coarse person has the best of it, after all. He repeats this main theme again and again in the poem, so that it is incredible that the critics did not see the point, even if they were right to condemn it. He says it plainly in the lines:

> No thorns go as deep as a rose's,
> And love is more cruel than lust;
> Time turns the old days to derision,

Our loves into corpses and wives,
And marriage and death and division
Make barren our lives.

And it is *then* only that he says, in words horrible enough, but with something of a moral horror:

And pale with the past we draw nigh thee
And satiate with comfortless hours:
And we know thee, how all men belie thee,
And we gather the fruit of thy flowers. . . .

Or again, elsewhere:

Of languors rekindled and rallied,
Of barren delights and unclean;
Things monstrous and fruitless; a pallid
And poisonous queen.

This is not praising sin, though it may be practising it. This is rather emphasizing the disgust that is the alternative to the disappointment. It is about as idolatrous as a disappointed lover talking to a bottle of gin, and saying, "Damn your ugly face, I believe you're my only friend, after all!"

I have dwelt a little on this particular point about

the poet, because it involves this very vital matter of the point about a poem. Even when it is understood, the attitude may be condemned—indeed, it should be condemned. But it should not be condemned for being something else. It is a morbid view, an unmanly view, a view immoral in its practical effects. But, above all, as seems to me most striking in this connexion, it is the very worst possible view of life for anybody proposing to raise a political revolution and to found a perfect Republic. That is the question which I asked first: why it is that men who seem so keen on reforming the world equip themselves with the worst possible philosophies for doing it? It is hard to say whether poor Swinburne was a more hopeless revolutionist in being a pessimist or in being an optimist. His pantheism could only prove that the worst things are good, because they are a part of nature; and his pessimism only proved that the best things are bad, because they are doomed to disappointment and sorrow. It seems either way a weak motive for dying on a barricade for the belief that one thing is better than another. We need a more fixed idea of truth to establish a reign of justice. But though Swinburne could hardly have given justice to men, he has a right to get justice from them. And I say this to show that on one point he did not receive justice—not even the justice that condemns.

III

"I have lived long enough to have seen one thing; that love hath an end"; so runs, as every one will remember, the first line of Swinburne's beautiful "Hymn to Proserpine," the dirge of a Pagan farewell to Paganism. I have lived long enough to have seen one thing: that the love of Swinburne hath an end. Not the admiration for Swinburne, not the reasonable appreciation of Swinburne; but that particular sort of love of Swinburne which is like first love in youth; perhaps (one is sometimes tempted to think) the only sort of real love that Swinburne had ever known anything about. I mean that sort of mere magic spell or enchantment by Swinburne which so many young people had in the period when, as Mr. Maurice Baring has very truly said, Swinburne seems to them not so much the best poet as simply the only poet. That sort of love certainly hath an end, and most of us have lived long enough to have seen it. But it is symbolic of something larger; something that is connected not only with Swinburne but with Swinburnianism.

Any man who has "lived long enough," and not actually stiffened with negative prejudices, must know by this time that the modern movement, and every sort of movement, revolves round and round the central pillar of the old Christian tradition. It is emphatically *not* leaving that pillar behind and rushing right away towards some other winning-post. He knows it, for the perfectly simple reason that he has seen it careering in two totally opposite directions, and neither of them has succeeded in getting away from the post. He knows by this time, if he is honest with himself, that the whole thing is like a Giddy-go-Round at a country fair; full of rush and romantic enjoyment, but revolving upon one centre that supports all the movement by being immovable. It is a glorious experience for children, and therefore for poets, who share some of the wisdom of children. It consists of concentric rings of hobby-horses, and a hobby-horse, like a hobby, is a very good thing to make a thinking man happy. In most Giddy-go-Rounds there are outer and inner rings of horses, nearer or farther from the centre; and this also is an allegory. In some Giddy-go-Rounds there are revolving rings going opposite ways which greatly increase the godlike quality of giddiness. In youth or childhood especially it is quite natural to be giddy, even if it sometimes begins to approximate to being sick. Of recent literature we might not unfairly say that for the first half of the time most of the modern poets were giddy; and now, in the second half of the time, most of the modern poets are sick.

Anyhow, Swinburne certainly rode his hobby-horse with great fire and galloping energy; but, when he fancied that he was leaving the central pillar of his childhood and his ancestry far behind him, he was really very far from the truth and very close to the pillar. And this is proved by the fact that both poetical and political energy has since galloped in exactly the contrary direction, and is still at about the same distance from the ancestral pillar as before. If anything, the more recent poets have tended to take their seats in the ring rather nearer to the pillar. I imagine that, if a man had gone round during the last ten years asking the young people in the literary world whom they regarded as their hope and hero and leader, as the young of my youth regarded Swinburne, it is about ten to one that most of them would mention Mr. T. S. Eliot. Wilde said that Swinburne was the only true Laureate, for the poet praised by all other poets must always wear the laurel. Laurels and Laureates are not so much in the style of our more cynical and realistic time. But the young would probably support a young writer like Mr. Eliot, even if both the young writer and the young admirers strike older people as being rather prematurely old. Anyhow, the two poets will serve very well for the purpose of the parallel about poetry, or even about politics.

Swinburne was quite certain that he and the world were galloping nearer and nearer to the new Republic and farther and farther from the old Church. If he had been right, it would follow that, by this time, a man like Mr. Eliot would be even more Republican than Swinburne. As a matter of fact, Mr. Eliot has actually walked out of a real live Republic and loudly announced that he is a Royalist. He has also declared himself an Anglo-Catholic; but I will leave the religious issue as far as possible on one side, because though even more cogent, it is much more controversial. But even in the matter of politics alone it is quite obvious that there has been a complete turn of the tide. The Giddy-go-Round is going round in the reverse direction, but, I am glad to say, almost as giddily. The wooden horses are galloping with their accustomed fervour, and I hope the children who ride on them are happy. But one who has seen this complete reversal of direction since his own childhood will not be able to believe that the horses broke loose from the post and fled farther and farther from it for ever merely because he was told so in childhood. Swinburne's hobby-horse, for instance, had a perpetual impulse to gallop away over the Alps into Italy. But suppose he were really still galloping into Italy, like

Hannibal or Napoleon, what sort of Italy would he find? The political ideas of Swinburne were the ideas of the period of Mazzini. The political ideas of T. S. Eliot are the ideas of the period of Mussolini. It might be maintained that the new poet is nearer than the old poet to the old Roman pillar of the past. It is stark nonsense to pretend that he is farther away.

I am not dealing directly here with things that I myself accept or reject. Many people know that my own religion is even more Roman than Mr. Eliot's. Yet in many ways my politics are much more Republican than Mr. Eliot's; perhaps much more really Republican than Swinburne's. But I am not arguing about what is right or wrong in any of these views. I am merely remarking on an actual revolution in the ideas of a large number of other people, and noting that it is more like the real revolution of a Giddy-go-Round than the mere riot of a gallop. In one sense it has been revolution against revolution; that is, revolution in one sense reversing revolution in the other. But nobody who notes the real movements in the intellectual world just now can doubt that there has been the sort of revolution that is called a reaction. In every country there has been a reaction, either practical or theoretical, in the direction of order or authority or classical proportion. In France there has been the influence of Maurras in politics or Maritain in religion. In Germany the Dictator is a vision; in Italy he is a fact. In America, the very last place where most people would look for classicism, there has arisen an influential school of classicists. Those who most fiercely denounce the fact most clearly confess the fact, and even their denunciations are witness that it is a universal fact. The enemies of Humanism denounce it as intellectual Fascism. The enemies of Fascism make fun of its appeal to classicism. Of course a man may quite reasonably like some of these things and dislike others, or like some parts of these things and dislike others, as I do myself. But, as I say, I am not talking about likes or dislikes, and I am not talking about myself. I am talking about the way the world goes round, and pointing out that the moral world does not always go round from right to left. It is, at this moment, most certainly going round from left to right. The sort of political party that used to be called the Extreme Right contains more of the really original modern thinkers than the party called the Extreme Left. I only say that the return to traditionalism is obviously strong enough to be recognized. I think it very possible that it may soon be strong enough to be resisted. But when strange survivals of the Swinburnian epoch, imagining themselves to be young, actually come and tell me that the world is on an endless march towards wild liberty and indefinite relaxation of everything, I really do not know how to answer, except with a melancholy smile. "I have lived long enough to have seen one thing . . ."

THE END